*Peter Sandiford
Memorial Lectures*
I
SOME ASPECTS OF EDUCATION
IN DENMARK

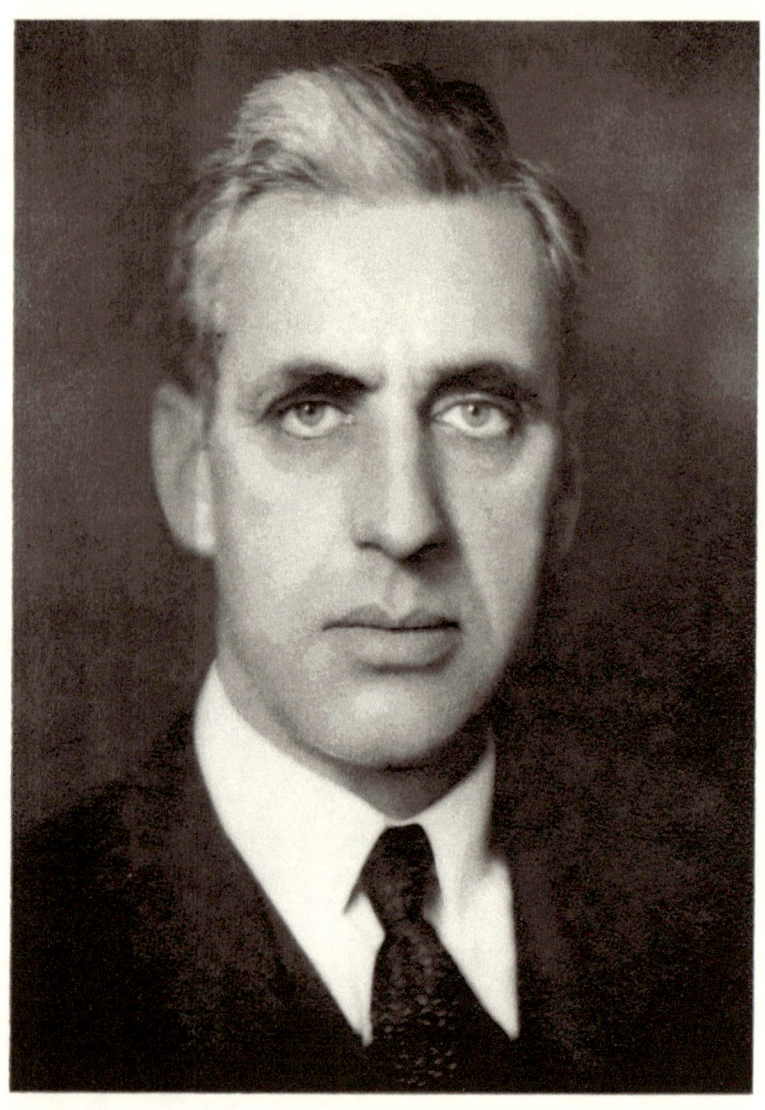

Peter Sandiford

OLE B. THOMSEN

Some Aspects of Education in Denmark

PUBLISHED FOR

The Ontario Institute for Studies in Education

BY

University of Toronto Press

© University of Toronto Press 1967
Printed in Canada
Reprinted in 2018
ISBN 978-1-4875-7349-2 (paper)

THE ONTARIO INSTITUTE FOR STUDIES IN EDUCATION is a college chartered by an Act of the Ontario Legislature in June, 1965. Its purpose is to study matters and problems relating to education, to disseminate the results of and assist in the implementation of the findings of educational studies; and to expand graduate instruction in education. The Institute is affiliated with the University of Toronto for degree-granting purposes.

Foreword

THE HONOURABLE MR. JUSTICE BORA LASKIN
Chairman of the Board of Governors
The Ontario Institute for Studies in Education

THE LECTURES published in this volume are the first-fruits of the Peter Sandiford Visiting Professorship, recently established by the Board of Governors of The Ontario Institute for Studies in Education. The Visiting Professorship, tenable for a period not exceeding one academic year, is a tribute to the memory of the late Dr. Peter Sandiford, who inspired the creation in 1931 of the Department of Educational Research in the Ontario College of Education, and was its first director. It is also a recognition of the Institute's appreciation of the importance of research in education, to which Dr. Sandiford gave unstinting devotion. Indeed, the Department of Educational Research has merged in the Institute, and the work it formerly carried on is now one of the Institute's major functions.

The Visiting Professor may, by arrangement, carry on research and teaching during his incumbency, but the one formal requirement of an appointment is the delivery of a series of public lectures which may thereafter be published by the Institute. Professor Ole B. Thomsen, at present Fellow of Higher Education in the University of Copenhagen, Denmark, has admirably discharged this obligation as the first Peter Sandiford Visiting Professor. I am pleased on behalf of the Board to welcome his contribution to the work of the Institute and am confident that it will reach a wide audience.

Contents

FOREWORD   v

INTRODUCTION   ix

FIRST LECTURE: *Recent Trends in Secondary Education*   1

    Roots of the Danish Education System, 4
    Eighteenth and Nineteenth Century School
      Legislation, 8
    The Education System Before the Reform of 1958, 12
    The Education System Since the Reform of 1958, 15
        The Folkschool, 18
        The *Real* Department, 23
        The Gymnasium, 24
        Organization of the Schoolwork, 28
        Examinations in Secondary Schools, 28
        Teacher Training for Primary and Lower
          Secondary Education, 29
    Concluding Remarks, 31

SECOND LECTURE: *Technical Education and Trade Training* 33
   Denmark: The Country and The People, 36
   The Transition from School to Productive Life, 40
   Apprenticeship in Trade and Industry, 42
   Advanced Training Based on Completed Apprenticeship, 44
   New Technical Courses, 46
   Commercial Education, 47
   Agricultural Training, 51
   The Problem of the Unskilled Worker, 52
   Educational Planning as an Agent in Social Change, 53

THIRD LECTURE: *Post-Secondary Education* 55
   The Danish Concept of Higher Education, 57
   The Universities, 61
      Entry Requirements, 63
      Degrees and Courses, 65
      Instruction and Examinations, 68
      The Danish Doctorate, 71
      University Teachers and Research Staff, 72
      An Attempt at Comparison, 74
   Other Institutions of Higher Education, 75
   The Future: Planning for Change and Expansion, 77

FOURTH LECTURE: *Adult Education* 83
   The Folk High School, 85
      The Origin of the Folk High School Movement, 86
      The Contributions of Kristen Kold, 90
      Impact of the Folk High School, 92
      Organization and Courses, 93
      The Folk High School in a Changing Society, 96
      The Folk High School in Other Countries, 98
   The Danish Evening School, 98
      The Evening School and the Future, 101
      The People's University and Boarding Schools for Youth, 102
   Concluding Remarks, 104

RECOMMENDED READINGS IN ENGLISH ON DANISH EDUCATION 107

Introduction

R. W. B. JACKSON
Director
The Ontario Institute for Studies in Education

THIS SERIES of four lectures was given by Ole B. Thomsen, first Peter Sandiford Visiting Professor at The Ontario Institute for Studies in Education, during the month of April 1966. In these lectures Professor Thomsen surveys the course of Danish education, focusing particularly on the secondary, post-secondary, and adult levels. What he says should be of considerable interest to Canadian and American educators. Denmark, although small in area and population, is important in the world of education. The Danes were showing concern about "education for all" at a time when Jacques Cartier was making his voyage of discovery along the St. Lawrence. In 1539, seventy-five years before the Recollet Fathers set up the first school on Canadian soil, Denmark passed an Ordinance decreeing that a school be organized in every town. In 1814 the Danish Government made education compulsory for all children from seven to fourteen years of age, thus placing itself in the vanguard of popular education.

Clearly, a country where such important decisions were made so early has a great deal to offer, and there is much in these lectures that we can read with profit. However, as Professor Thomsen points out early in his first lecture, we must also read with care. What has been successful in Danish education might not work well here. We must understand that an education system does not develop in a vacuum, but rather in response to certain conditions in a particular society at a particular time. Since no system can be adequately understood without some knowledge of these conditions, Professor Thomsen devotes several pages to putting his country's education system in historical perspective.

The author is in an advantageous position to describe Danish education. He is a product of Danish elementary and secondary schools and has studied both law and educational theory at the University of Copenhagen, graduating with a *cand. jur.* degree in 1960 and a *cand. art.* in 1965. He has studied in Switzerland and the United Kingdom, lectured in political science in the University of Copenhagen, and taught labour law and sociology in the Copenhagen School of Economics and Social Science. Professor Thomsen's experience also includes a year as a primary school teacher and seven years' night school teaching at the Municipal Youth School of Copenhagen. As a student, Professor Thomsen held the posts of president and vice-president of Denmark's National Union of Students.

From 1960 to December, 1965, Professor Thomsen was secretary in the Department for Higher Education in the Danish Ministry of Education. During this period he served as secretary of several committees concerned with higher education and educational planning. He now holds the posi-

Introduction xi

tion of Fellow of Higher Education in the University of Copenhagen.

During his six months at OISE, Professor Thomsen was attached to the Division of Educational Planning. As part of the Division's teaching program he conducted an educational planning course which was the first of its kind offered in schools of education.

Professor Thomsen's lectures should be read as accounts of particular Danish answers to questions confronting educators in North America as well. The first lecture, for example, deals with the structure of the secondary school system and the thorny problems involved in educating the non-academic student. The second lecture, on technical education and trade training, describes Denmark's transition from an agrarian to an industrialized society, and the resulting alterations in the education system. Professor Thomsen also discusses the role of the apprenticeship system, and the growing need for technicians—both important subjects to educators in Canada who are trying to cope with the increasing demand for highly skilled workers.

In the third lecture, where Professor Thomsen is dealing with his specialty, higher education, his comments are of especial value. Although he presents a system completely different from that to which we are accustomed in North America, at the same time he discusses such familiar and contentious matters as free university education, student support, overcrowded lecture halls, and the shape of new universities.

The final lecture concerns an area still relatively unexplored in Canada, adult education. In this lecture Professor Thomsen describes the ideals and achievements of N. F. S. Grundtvig, the remarkable thinker who sought to strengthen democracy in Denmark by providing advanced general education for the common, non-academic man. Grundtvig's influence led to the formation of Folk High Schools and Evening Schools throughout the country, and developed leaders in communal affairs. His achievements furnish us with an example we might find useful in North America, where the increase in leisure time seems accompanied by the individual's inability to use it either to his own or to the community's advantage. Leaders in developing nations, faced with acute problems in teaching their citizens the ways of democracy, are also finding it profitable to study Denmark's system of adult education.

In the years ahead, we in Canada will be faced with serious decisions about the directions our education systems ought to take. We can learn much from the experience of countries which, like Denmark, were providing answers while we were still in the process of discovering what the questions were.

FIRST LECTURE

*Recent Trends
in Secondary Education*

Recent Trends
in Secondary Education

IT HAS BECOME POPULAR recently to study the education systems of other countries. Often such studies are motivated by the prospect of borrowing useful elements that one might want to transplant to one's own schools. It is a quite acceptable motive; there is no reason to look down upon it. The problems most of us are facing at this moment, problems of adapting our education to the fast-changing needs of society, are too immense for any country to solve on its own. But we have to remind ourselves that any transplantation on a living organism may be perilous. It has to be done with a careful understanding of the conditions under which the transplanted part functions in its natural environment. So it is with educational borrowing. Comparing education systems in isolation from their historical, social, and ideological context tends to be meaningless. For such comparison to be of any value, one should therefore not study just *what* they are. It is just as essential to understand *why* and *how* they became what they are.

Because this understanding is essential, I will ask your patience while I trace back to their origin at least a couple of roots of the present organization of the schools in Denmark. Some knowledge of our history should help you to see our education system in clearer perspective.

ROOTS OF THE DANISH EDUCATION SYSTEM

The roots of Danish education grow deep in the soil of history. The oldest of the existing schools in Denmark can be traced back to the twelfth and thirteenth centuries.[1] Our tradition of compulsory education for all children is older than that of most other countries.[2] Perhaps these deep roots make our schools more resistant to frequent changes. They are not inclined to waver before the breezes of suggested change; most often only a gale will get them moving. On the other hand, there is strength in a long historic tradition. Old trees often bloom earlier than the young.

Many factors may be pointed out as essential to explain the process whereby Danish education grew into what it is today, for good and for ill. But there are two features that seem to me, as I review our education history, to stand out clearly. Both of them provide a clue for the foreign observer who tries to understand some fundamental aspects of our present education system.

---

1. Willis Dixon, *Education in Denmark* (Copenhagen: Centraltrykkeriet, 1958), p. 9. The historical account given in this lecture is mainly based on Dixon's work, but occasionally also on Aksel Nellemann, *Schools and Education in Denmark*, trans. John B. Powell ("Danish Information Handbooks"; Copenhagen: Det Danske Selskab, 1964), and on K. Ottosen, *Vor Folkeskoles Oprindelse og Udvikling* (Copenhagen: Glydendal, 1931).

2. K. Grue-Sørensen, *Opdragelsens Historie* (Copenhagen: Gyldendal, 1959), III, 146–76.

Recent Trends in Secondary Education

The first of these features is that in Denmark education very early came to be regarded as a concern of the state, and has constantly remained so.[3] The second is that for more than four hundred years there seems to have been just as much concern about primary education for most of the population as there was for academic secondary education for the selected minority. There is ample evidence in history to justify these sweeping generalizations.

During the years when Denmark was Catholic, that is, up to 1536, schools were entirely under the control of the Church and were Latin Schools designed mainly to fulfil the Church's needs. In a number of townships, reading and writing schools existed as well, set up by townspeople to meet the requirements of commercial life. These schools were never very numerous in Denmark.

The first attempt to introduce popular education was made by King Christian II in 1521, a few years before the collapse of the Roman Catholic Church in Denmark. In a letter that year he ordered that "peasants who wish to have their children instructed should send them to the parish priest, deacon or other person, who can teach them the Creed, Lord's Prayer and 'Hail Mary', in Danish, and also teach them to read and write their mother tongue."[4] This provision was intended for the rural districts. Townsfolk, on their part, "should see that they get a schoolmaster from the University or they should themselves teach the children their letters, the Lord's Prayer and 'Hail Mary', together with reading and writing Danish and reckoning." It was a very ambitious plan, too ambitious to be implemented. (So too, it seems, were other of the King's plans, for shortly afterwards he was forced to leave the throne to spend the rest of his life in prison.) Although this well-intentioned plan

---

3. For a discussion of the role of the Ministry of Education and of centralized control over education in Denmark, see Dixon, *op. cit.*, p. 171 and pp. 189–92.
4. In Dixon's translation, *op. cit.*, p. 10.

for the extension of education to all children never came into force, it clearly demonstrates that the government, even at a relatively early period, felt responsible for education and for popular education in particular.

Eighteen years later a new Church Ordinance also comprising regulations about the schools was promulgated. That was in 1539, three years after the Reformation had transferred to the Danish king the highest authority in affairs previously under the control of the pope. The Ordinance decreed that, in each town, one school be set up graded into four classes where teacher requirements for such grading could be met. The dichotomy between the clerical Latin School and the secular reading and writing school was abolished, as it was intended that there be only one school in each town, and that a Latin School. This school, however, should provide elementary and secondary education for all children in the town.

The Ordinance did not prescribe compulsory school attendance. But it did make a strong plea for the parish parsons to urge people to send their children to school, "so that by training and teaching it is possible to produce persons for Church and State." The town school, as it was established by the Ordinance, was strikingly similar to today's school organization. It was a comprehensive school in that all children went to the same school and received the same kind of instruction. The school was unstreamed till the age of twelve-plus, when the first selection took place. But let the document speak for itself: "Likewise should the schoolmasters with all diligence pay attention to the pupils' aptitude and always, when the children are over their twelfth year, give the parents a true estimate for knowing which of the pupils are not thought likely to make progress, so that in time they may be set elsewhere to something else. But those who have ability should be kept in the school until their sixteenth year." At this age a new streaming should take place between those "who can with profit share with others what they have obtained from their studies, and those who are thought able to do this should be offered to the service of God and sent to the University," whereas those "who cannot so well profit must be taken from the school and set to honest, worldly occupations."[5]

Serious steps were taken to ensure that the reform was put into effect. State leaders, realizing that the implementation of the Ordinance depended on economic resources, used confiscated Church revenues and endowments to help maintain the schools. About sixty such schools were established in the years after the Ordinance. Not all of them survived economically, and not all of them observed fully the spirit of the Ordinance. Still, they formed a pattern whose most essential features are still kept alive in the physiognomy of our schools up to this very day.

You will remember that this school was only for town children. The children in rural areas, however, were not forgotten by the Ordinance. Since at that time it was not practicable to organize a stable school system for these districts, the parish deacon was to teach children in rural parishes. This proved to be an unsatisfactory arrangement. School buildings and well-educated deacons were both in short supply, and farmers were negligent in sending their children to the school. But at least a beginning was made. A principle was established, and in the course of the following centuries a great number of schools were built through the country. Thus was established the institution of the schoolmaster-deacon, which has made one of the most colourful contributions to our educational history,[6] and has had a very strong bearing on the educational development in rural areas up to the present.

5. Dixon, *op. cit.*, p. 11.
6. See, for instance, Georg Hansen's amusing study *Degnen* (Copenhagen, 1944). The schoolmaster-deacon has been immortalized by the character Peer Degn in Ludvig Holberg's comedy *Erasmus Montanus*.

The Ordinance of 1539 was the first important milestone in our history of education. We should note here that although supervision of the schools was left to the national church there was no doubt that education was the concern of the state. Organizing, maintaining, and legislating for the schools was clearly a responsibility of the government. It is also significant that provisions were made for common elementary education as well as for secondary education.

EIGHTEENTH- AND NINETEENTH-CENTURY SCHOOL LEGISLATION

Two hundred years later, the Pietism movement was instrumental in bringing Danish education to its second important milestone. This was the Education Act of 1739.[7] Since educational provisions for rural areas had been far from satisfying, the Act ordered, "All children in the school-district, who are over five or six years of age and can come to school, ought to come to school diligently for as long as possible; but at plough and harvest-time, the children may be out of school."[8] Every deacon was to "hold" a school, and certain conditions were set up regarding qualifications for becoming a deacon. Children should stay at school at least until they could read and knew their Christian learning. Although education was not yet made compulsory, there was a unique spur to attend school. This was the institution of compulsory Confirmation, introduced in 1736, which dictated that no one could be confirmed unless he had been sent to read and be instructed in the necessary works of Christian learning. Confirmation was an indispensable condition for getting married.[9] So no schooling

7. Forordning om Skolerne paa Landet i Danmark og hvad Degnene og Skoleholderne derfor maa nyde, 23 Jan., 1739.
8. Dixon's translation, *op. cit.*, p. 24.
9. Ottosen, *op. cit.*, p. 33.

meant no Confirmation, and no Confirmation meant no marriage. A heavy responsibility logically rested on parents who neglected to send their children to school.

While the state began to prepare in this way for the next step, the introduction of compulsory education for all, a reform of the town schools was carried out through laws of 1739 and 1756. More than half the existing Latin Schools were abolished in order to secure satisfactory economic conditions for the remainder. For the same reason, the lower grades of these schools were cut off, and it was required that the children who entered the Latin School be able to read and write Danish and have some command of Latin. The Latin School thus became a secondary school. A dualistic school system was introduced to replace the old "unity school." A later age would deplore the separation.

Toward the ending of the eighteenth century, Denmark's first teacher training colleges were set up.[10] Their founding was part of a far-reaching educational reform carried out over a period of twenty-five years by the Great School Committee. The Committee's efforts led to another major step in 1814, the most decisive year in Danish school history. This was the year that education was made compulsory for all children from seven years of age until Confirmation at about the age of fourteen.[11] I do not intend to go into detail about this important reform.[12] I should only like to point out that the impact of this law cannot be overestimated, especially as it relates to rural districts. This law was marked by such foresight that up to 1937 it was still the

10. The first teacher training college within the borders of the kingdom was established under the supervision of the Great School Committee at Blaagaard in Copenhagen in 1791. It was followed in subsequent years by teacher training colleges at: Brahetrolleborg, 1793; Vesterborg, 1802; Brøndbyvester, 1802; Skaarup, 1803; and Borris, 1806.
11. Anordning for Almueskolevæsenet paa Landet i Danmark, 29 Juli, 1814.
12. See Dixon, *op. cit.*, pp. 48–56.

main law for schools in rural areas. It was so far ahead of its time that many of its instructions[13] to teachers about the spirit of classroom practices are still consistent with the most advanced pedagogical thinking.

While in the first part of the nineteenth century attention was focused on elementary schooling, the second half was devoted to major reforms within secondary schools. Long before the middle of the century, the rudiments of the present *Real* department had been set up as an alternative course to the Latin School. Our word *Real* indicates a relationship to real life. Accordingly, this course was designed to meet the need for secondary education in modern languages, mathematics, and the rapidly emerging sciences, subjects that were stubbornly neglected by the traditional Latin School. The course was more in keeping with the needs and attitudes of the increasingly influential bourgeois class, and was made the general entrance requirement for the Technical University which had been set up in 1829.

But the Latin School had to change too. Its curriculum had to be reformed and its connection with the elementary school re-established. Curriculum reforms were instituted by laws of 1850[14] and 1871.[15] Gradually, modern languages and science were conceded a place in the Latin School. In 1903 all the parts of the school system, the elementary school, the *Real* department, and the Latin School were joined into one unified school system.[16] The same year the Gymnasium, i.e., the upper three years of the old Latin School, was finally split up into three departments: one for classical languages, one for modern languages, and one for science.

13. Instruction for Lærerne i Almueskolerne paa Landet i Danmark (Appendix A).
14. Madvig'ske Skolelov af 13 Maj, 1850.
15. Hall'ske Skolelov, 1 Ap., 1871.
16. Lov om Højere Almenskoler, 24 Ap., 1903.

These, then, are the historic roots of our schools. You will have noticed that from very early times development has been directed by laws indicating the interest and unquestioned authority of the state in educational affairs. The degree to which schools in Denmark are directed by the central authority often surprises foreigners. But the foregoing has given you the historical explanation. It also explains why we have reached certain educational milestones before other countries, and why change—when it is decided upon—can be directed into all schools in the country without insurmountable complications. We have not had to await the settlement of strife over education between church and state or between different churches to implement common education. And we do not have to convince each local board of education in order to put into practice curricular or other reforms.

An explanation of our traditional deep concern about educational opportunities for youngsters who are not expected to advance to academic education must also be sought in history. Our popular education was originally designed for a population with a majority of farmers, whereas other school systems have been constructed to meet the growing demands of industry. In large segments of our population there has always been some scepticism about academic education and so our educational system has had to adapt itself also to the needs and culture of those who intended to enter farming or the trades after school was over. Why should they be deprived of educational opportunities that within their scope could match the academic stream of the schools? Why should they be pressed into an academic mould that did not suit their capacities, interests, and occupational needs? This is the historic question behind the discussions about the non-examination department of the secondary school.

THE EDUCATION SYSTEM BEFORE THE REFORM OF 1958

The organization of our schools today is based on two laws of 1958. One of them deals with the Folkschool,[17] which normally comprises Grades 1 through 10, the other with the Gymnasium,[18] the three-year course that leads to entrance to the universities and other institutions of higher learning.

To show the changes these laws brought about, let me briefly describe our previous school system. Before 1958, the ordinary rural school comprised the seven grades that correspond to the age groups of compulsory education. The typical town school consisted of a five-year *Grundskole*, followed by a four-year Middle School and a one-year *Real* department.

In that system the Middle School began at Grade 6 and was divided into an examination department and a non-examination department. The selection of department after Grade 5 was based on written tests in the basic subjects of the *Grundskole*. The non-examination department consisted mainly of the subjects of the *Grundskole* extended another two, three, or four years, depending on how long the youngsters stayed on beyond the statutory school-leaving age, which was then fourteen. There would not be any sort of examination in this part of the school. The examination department was somewhat more academic in content and was concluded, after four years, by the Middle School Examination. After passing the Middle School Examination the youngsters could continue another year in the *Real* department and sit for the *Realeksamen* at the end of that year. The most talented of them, however, might enter the Gymnasium immediately after the Middle School Examina-

17. Lovbekendtgørelse nr. 220 af 18 Juni, 1958 om Folkeskolen.
18. Lov nr. 165 af 7 Juni, 1958 om Gymnasieskoler.

tion, though some of them would, for safety's sake, first take the *Realeksamen.*

The Gymnasium offered a broad liberal arts curriculum on a fairly high academic level. It aimed at giving those who could profit from such instruction an advanced general education which was valuable in itself. Equally important, the Gymnasium led to the *Studentereksamen*, which was the accepted entrance requirement of universities and other institutions of higher learning. The Gymnasium was separated into three branches: classics, science, and modern languages. All three had roughly the same subjects in their curriculum. The difference was that the number of periods per week in some subjects varied from branch to branch, thus creating a variation in emphasis.

This was the structure of the Danish education system before 1958. In several ways it was not satisfactory. The non-examination Middle School in particular was the object of widespread discontent. This department, introduced in 1937, had never had the success that was hoped for it. Although vigorous attempts were made to apply modern theories of education to curriculum and instructional techniques, this part of the Middle School did not work out well. The basic difficulty was that it lacked a content of its own. It did not seem to lead anywhere. Naturally, parents who wanted their children to advance did everything possible to get them into the examination Middle School.

As a result, the latter department, which was originally designed for only one fourth of all children, soon had to accommodate half of each age group.[19] This development had two effects. First, the standard of the Middle School Examination was seriously threatened, since it gradually adapted itself to students for whom it was never intended. Second, and perhaps more serious, the non-examination

19. K. Grue-Sørensen, *op. cit.*, p. 294.

department came to be considered not as something positive in itself, but merely as a place for children not good enough for the examination department. This "downgrading" of the non-examination department naturally affected the teachers' and the students' attitudes to it. They grew increasingly apathetic, and the general negative attitude spread to employers, who increasingly demanded at least Middle School Examination or preferably *Realeksamen* for employment in even the simplest jobs or apprenticeships. It was quite obvious that nothing but a total reorganization of the Middle School would serve if adequate provision were to be made for the unfortunate proportion of youngsters who, at the end of Grade 5, did not pass that fateful entrance examination to the examination Middle School.

There were other reasons why reform was necessary in 1958. For centuries the educational opportunities of town children and children in rural areas had been highly unequal. The typical seven-year school in rural areas did not give the children adequate opportunities for entering the path that led to the *Real-* and *Studentereksamen*, or to education that in other ways might suit their needs. These inequalities were recognized, and for years demands had been made that rural children have access to the same instruction as their contemporaries in the towns.

Liberal elements in the population were calling also for the establishment of a comprehensive unstreamed school system for all children within the age group of compulsory education.[20] Although there was wide disagreement as to the feasibility of such an unstreamed school, the matter had been discussed for so long that it was felt to be ready for a

---

20. For a systematic exposition in condensed form of the ideas behind the comprehensive school, see Ole B. Thomsen, "Educational Change in Scandinavia" in *New Dimensions in Curriculum Development*, The Proceedings of the Second International Curriculum Conference, Toronto, Canada, February 8–11, 1966 (Toronto: The Ontario Curriculum Institute, 1966), pp. 39–47.

final test in Parliament. In the same way, the contention about raising the school-leaving age to somewhere above fourteen was due to be moved to the floor of Parliament. Concurrent demands for abolishing all examinations in the Folkschool could be included in Parliamentary debates.

Few laws have been brought into the world with sharper birth pangs than the law of 1958 concerning Folkschools. When a bill was first proposed in Parliament in 1955 it quickly became evident that the parties were far too remote from each other on the crucial points mentioned above to agree on a far-reaching reform of the school system. It is a tradition in Denmark that an educational issue should not become a political football, but that education acts should be backed by a united Parliament. As a result, there ensued a period of painstaking negotiations, withdrawals of proposed bills and tabling of new ones, until finally a none too satisfactory compromise was reached in the Folkschool Law of 1958. Figures 1 and 2 show in rough outline the education system in Denmark before 1958 and after the reform of that year.

THE EDUCATION SYSTEM SINCE THE REFORM OF 1958

No change in the school-leaving age was introduced. The child is still to be instructed from the school year in which he completes his seventh year until the end of the school year in which he completes his fourteenth year.[21] This does not mean that children must go to school, only that they must receive instruction. It has always been the rule in Danish education that parents are free to send their children to school, be it public or private, or make other proper provision for their instruction. This rule was originally in keeping with Lutheran emphasis on the educative functions of

---

21. Lov om Folkeskolen, para. 43.

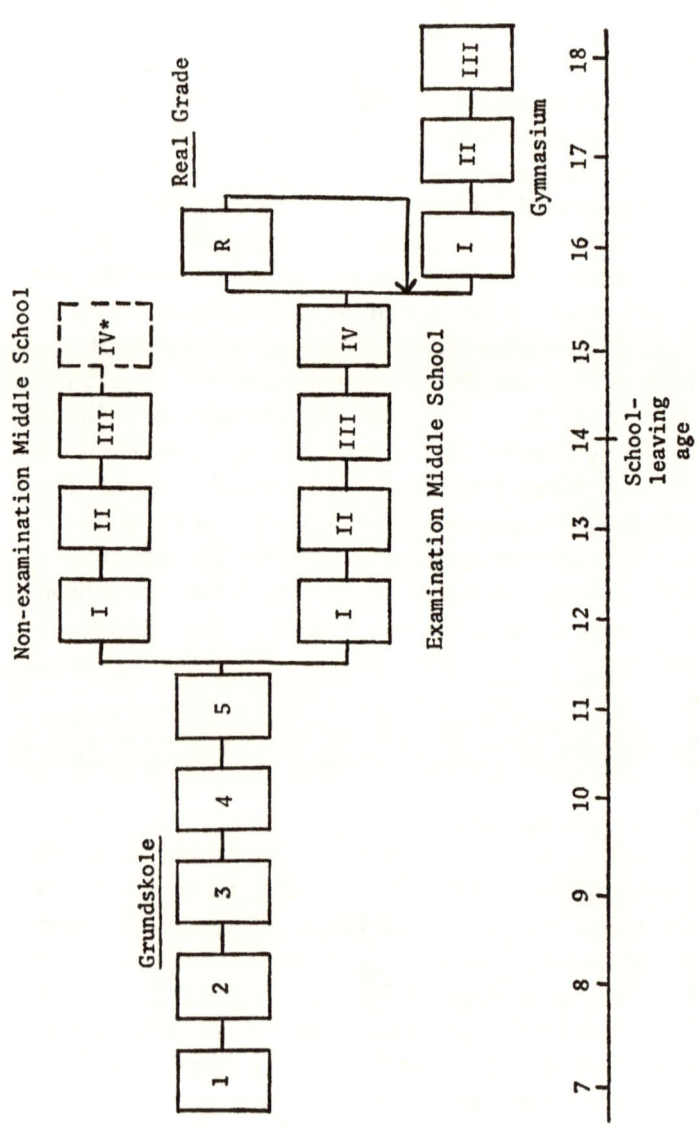

FIGURE 1. The organizational structure of a typical urban school before 1958.

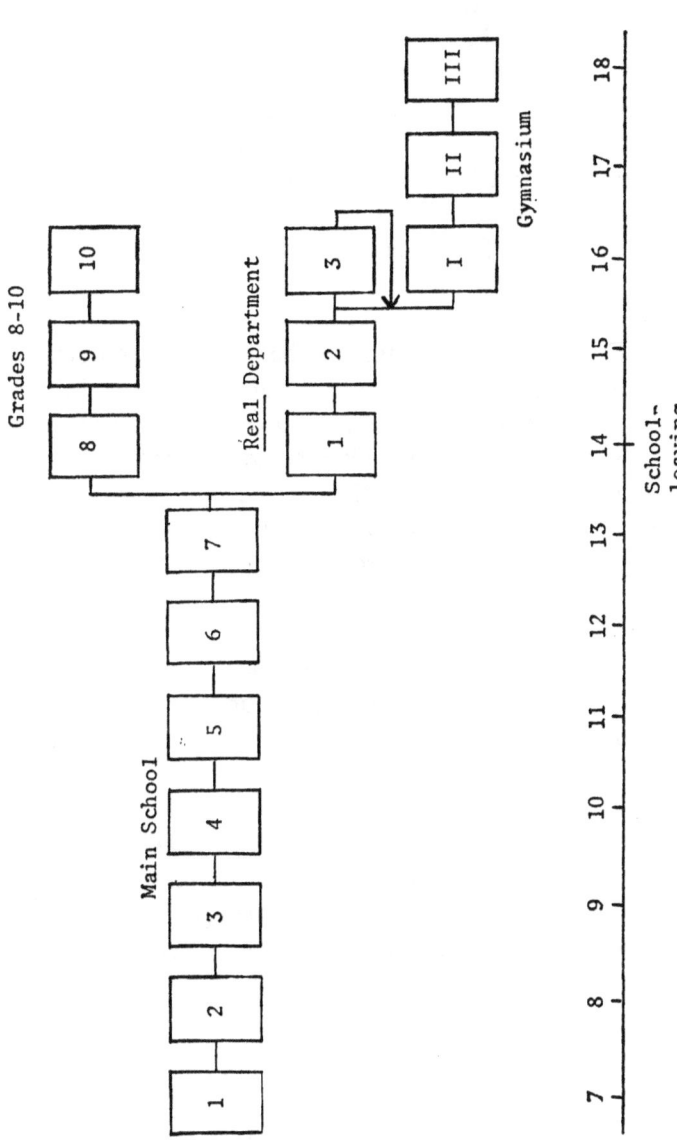

FIGURE 2. Rough outline of the present organizational structure of the elementary and secondary school level in Denmark.

the family, and was later reinforced by Grundtvigian[22] scepticism about state interference in education. Only a small minority of parents in Denmark actually prefer to instruct their children themselves, usually up to Grade 2 or 3, after which the children attend school. Out of 563,000 children in the compulsory education age in 1960, only 220 received such tuition at home. Yet the principle has survived unattacked for more than four hundred years.

The Folkschool

The Folkschool, according to the law, is a municipal school and consists of a seven- or eight-year Main School (*Hovedskole*), which may be extended by a 9th and 10th Grade. The Folkschool may also include a three-year *Real* department.[23] According to the new law there is no difference made in provisions for rural and urban areas.

In principle, the first seven years of the Main School is unstreamed and no examinations will be held in this period. The pupils advance through the grades according to their age, progress, maturity, and abilities. The subjects of the first five grades comprise the three R's, history, geography, biology, religion, physical exercises, music, and creative arts.[24] In Grades 6 and 7 the curriculum is extended to include science, woodworking and domestic science, and one foreign language, ordinarily English.[25] Some instruction should be given in Swedish and Norwegian in connection with the study of Danish. In Grade 7 mathematics and a second foreign language, ordinarily German, are offered to pupils who can profit from them. Pupils who want to go on to the *Real* department after Grade 7 are normally required to have taken the second foreign language in Grade 7.[26]

A concession to the opponents of the unstreamed school

22. N. F. S. Grundvig was the originator of the Danish Folk High School movement with its strong emphasis on independence in education.
23. Lov om Folkeskolen, paras. 1–2. 24. *Ibid.*, para. 17.1.
25. *Ibid.*, para. 17.2–3. 26. *Ibid.*, para. 20

is found in the so-called "mild" streaming that may take place after Grade 5. The law prescribes that where a school has more than one class per grade the children will at the beginning of Grade 6 be divided into streams according to their "attainment, abilities, and interests."[27] The children will not be tested before this streaming. The school decides which stream will suit the child best on the basis of a general impression of the child, but with due attention to the expressed desires of the parents. Such streaming will normally lead to the establishment of two lines, the a-line and the b-line. The former is usually called the "general line" and the latter the "book line."

Local school authorities may decide, however, that their Grades 5 shall be continued unstreamed as so-called c-lines through Grades 6 and 7. In the same way, a majority of the parents of the children in a given Grade 5 may decide that the class shall not be streamed in the subsequent grades, but provision shall be made for a differentiated curriculum in Grade 7. Adherents of the unstreamed school are encouraged by the fact that a substantial number of school boards and parents have chosen the unstreamed alternative. Since 1958 the number of unstreamed classes in Grades 6 and 7 has been steadily increasing. In 1964–65, for example, 60 per cent of all Grade 6 classes were unstreamed, an increase from 55 per cent the previous year.[28] Even though the major part of this figure may be explained by many schools in rural districts being too small to allow streaming in Grades 6 and 7, it is apparent that the mild streaming has not solved the problem of selection. At present it seems likely that this will be one of the first points that will be attacked and probably changed by a new and more thorough school reform.

27. *Ibid.*, para. 17.7.
28. *Skole-, Klasse- og Elevstatistik 1964/65 for Folke- og Gymnasieskole* (Copenhagen: Undervisningsministeriet, 1965).

In most respects, it is justifiable to include our Grades 6 and 7 in what historical and comparative education considers secondary education. But what you term secondary education will more probably include our Grades 8 through 10, our *Real* department, and our Gymnasium. I shall therefore devote my remarks to these three departments of the school system.

Grades 8, 9, and 10, one department of our secondary education, constitute the most significant innovation in the entire complex of the Education Acts of 1958, although the law itself is not very specific at this particular point. It states merely that the instruction of Grade 7 is to be continued in Grades 8 through 10 with a special view to preparing pupils for general or technical youth education, and that a certain streaming may take place in the light of the pupils' future professional activities. These courses must not, however, become real trade training.[29]

The success these grades have had so far—and they have enjoyed considerable success—must be ascribed to the wise recommendations of the Curriculum Committee which was set up to advise school boards on the implementation of the law.[30] As far as Grades 8 through 10 are concerned, the Committee was determined not to repeat the errors of the unsuccessful Middle School. The Committee has endeavoured to give these grades a content of their own, and to fashion a curriculum that would attract the youngsters and restore the confidence of trade and industry in this department.

The local school authorities have been given a free hand in setting up these grades in the way they find feasible. Generally, they construct their curricula on the basis of

29. Lov om Folkeskolen, para. 17.4.
30. *Undervisningsvejledning for Folkeskolen*, Betænkning nr. 253 afgivet af det af Undervisningsministeriet under 1 September, 1958 nedsatte Læseplansudvalg (Copenhagen, 1962).

Recent Trends in Secondary Education 21

a nucleus of general subjects which all students have to take, and a number of optional subjects.[31] The general subjects may be Danish, including literature; writing; arithmetic and accounting; historical, geographical, and biological topics; subjects with social and vocational orientations. The optional subjects which the school offers will depend largely on local conditions and needs. They may be practical, like shopwork, woodwork, needlework, cooking, creative arts, typewriting, advanced bookkeeping, and agricultural sciences; or academic, like English, German, geography, biology, and mathematics. By the grouping together of such optional subjects, a number of lines will be established, for instance, agricultural, general housekeeping, commercial, clerical, technical, and various not too specialized trade lines. These lines were established with a view to preparing young people for vocational training, never to giving such training in itself. A small school, of course, will not be able to set up all these lines, but by co-operating with other municipalities most areas will be able to offer children a variety of courses suitable to their needs.

When children leave school after Grade 7, 8, 9, or 10, they receive a certificate that states which subjects they have studied after the fifth school year. The certificate also contains an evaluation—in words, not in marks—of their attainment in some of the basic subjects. The certificate also reports on the pupil's diligence, interests, and special aptitudes. This makes it possible to point out characteristics of the pupil which may be of value for an employer even though the pupil's standing in certain subjects may perhaps not be very high. In this way, every pupil who has shown interest and has been careful with his school work will be able to leave the school with a positive report.

In order to wipe out the scepticism that was previously

31. *Ibid.*, ch. 27, pp. 233–72.

attached to the non-examination Middle School, and to make the courses in Grades 8 to 10 acceptable to employers and institutions of further education, a voluntary "state-controlled examination" has also been instituted for this department of the Folkschool, which the pupils may take after Grade 9 or 10. It increases the value of their leaving certificate considerably if they do so. Some schools offer a line or course leading to the preliminary technical examination (*Teknisk Forberedelseseksamen*) after Grade 9, or to a more advanced technical examination (*Udvidet Teknisk Forberedelseseksamen*) after Grade 10. In this case, the leaving examination after Grade 9 or Grade 10 is designed to meet the requirement of this technical examination, which gives admission to advanced technical courses for technical assistants, laboratory technicians, and a number of trades that previously preferred Middle School or *Realeksamen* as entry requirements.

The new Grades 8–10 have existed for less than eight years. Their establishment has involved many difficulties. Shops and equipment which had not been common for schools were now required. The new practical subjects required teachers with a background not given by the teacher training colleges. And the whole idea was so new that every step had to be experimental to some degree. By virtue, however, of the immense goodwill with which this serious attempt to solve a grave problem was met, the new grades have now been established with considerable success. Trade and industry, business life, and government agencies have opened their doors to youngsters from these grades. Perhaps the best evidence of success is that twice as many children now enter Grade 8 as enter the first grade of the *Real* department.[32]

32. Cf. comment on pp. 13–14 respecting enrolment in the examination Middle School.

The Real Department

Let us turn next to the *Real* department.[33] Transfer to this department ordinarily takes place after Grade 7, irrespective of stream. But students who transfer are required to have had instruction in one foreign language in Grade 6 and in two foreign languages and mathematics in Grade 7. Students may also transfer from Grades 8 or 9 of the Folkschool. Transfer from any of these grades to the second or third year of the *Real* course may also be allowed, provided the student passes a test to prove he has attained a level comparable to that of students in the grade he wants to enter. The normal development, however, will be transfer after Grade 7. The general condition of entry to the *Real* department is that the pupil is mature enough and knows enough to be able to profit from and complete the *Real* course within the prescribed period. Judgment of this is made by the school where the pupil has been instructed up to this point. If the school does not consider him suited for the *Real* course, he may on request be given a test to prove his suitability.

The complete *Real* course lasts three years and will usually comprise the age groups fourteen–sixteen. Its curriculum includes Danish (with Norwegian and Swedish), English, German, French, mathematics, history (with civics), geography, biology, physics and chemistry, handwriting, arts, manual work, music, and physical training. Mathematics has six periods a week, Danish five or six, English from three to five, German three to four, whereas most of the other subjects have one to three periods. French is taught for only one or two years and is optional. Latin is offered the second or third year and is required of those who stay in a language branch of the Gymnasium. Sex education

33. Lov om Folkeskolen, paras. 19–22.

must be given. Religious education is not compulsory for pupils whose parents do not wish it.

An innovation is the technical stream which may be established in the third year of the *Real* course. This will emphasize mathematics and physics, and will lead to the technical *Realeksamen*.

The examination at the completion of the third year is both written and oral. A pass in this examination opens the door to positions in municipal administration, banking, insurance companies, business, shipping, etc., and to a wide variety of opportunities in further education. Some of the institutions of higher learning are also open to *Real* graduates, provided they pass a special entrance examination for which additional preparation of about one year is required.

The Gymnasium

As I pointed out in the historical account earlier, the Danish Gymnasium developed out of the old Latin School. In the nineteenth century the Gymnasium was remodelled by and large after the pattern of the German Gymnasium. In the middle of the century it was forced to include science, mathematics, and modern languages in its curriculum. At the same time the university abolished its first degree—a remnant of the bachelor's degree—and assigned to the Gymnasium the general liberal arts training on which the university would base its graduate education. Since that time Danish universities have not granted a bachelor's degree but give only professional and graduate courses of six to eight years' duration. Thus the Gymnasium has functions that may be said to parallel those of your liberal arts colleges. It gives advanced instruction in a broad field of the liberal arts with all the personal benefits that may be derived from that, and it provides the necessary basis for commencing scientific studies at the universities and other institutions of higher learning.[34] The certificate for having passed the *Studentereksamen* at the end of the Gymnasium course is the only legal entrance requirement of the universities in Denmark.[35] Although the Gymnasium has this double purpose, it is sought almost exclusively by those intending to enter an institution of higher learning afterwards: a general liberal arts education in itself has little professional function in Danish society. Almost one hundred per cent of our Gymnasium graduates therefore enter some field of advanced education.

It is necessary when making statistical comparisons to be aware of this difference between the North American high school and the Danish Gymnasium. There are a little more than four and a half million inhabitants in Denmark. Last year there were 36,000 students in 89 Gymnasiums.[36] The same year about 9,000 passed the *Studentereksamen*, which is about 10 per cent of the total number of eighteen- to nineteen-year-olds. The percentage of each generation who go through the Gymnasium has increased rapidly since 1950, when between only 2 and 3 per cent of all eighteen- to nineteen-year-olds passed the *Studentereksamen*. We expect this percentage to rise to about 14 by 1970. But still it is very low when compared to other countries. Part of the difference in figures between high school attendance in Canada and attendance at the Danish Gymnasium may also stem from the possibility that in Denmark the *Real* departments perform some functions which are undertaken in Canada by the high school, and that Denmark has such a well developed system of trade and technical education as an alternative to high school.

According to the law of 1958, the Gymnasium is divided into two lines, each with three branches. There is a language

34. Lov om Gymnasieskoler, para. 2.
35. *Ibid.*, para. 8.
36. *Skole-, Klasse- og Elevstatistik 1964/65 for Folke- og Gymnasieskole.*

line and a mathematical line. The language line is subdivided into branches for classical languages, modern languages, and languages combined with social science. The mathematical line is subdivided into branches for mathematics and physics, biology, and mathematics combined with social science. In each case the normal course lasts three years. As with the *Real* course, the Gymnasium course may be taken by older people who attend day or evening classes set up by the state, by municipalities, or on private initiative. In these cases the course is shortened to two years. About 10 per cent of all *Studentereksamens* are taken from such institutions.

Within each of the two main lines, the language and the mathematical, the curriculum is identical for the three branches in the first year of the course; 29 out of 36 weekly periods are common to each line.[87] This innovation in the Gymnasium law of 1958 is in keeping with the general view that specialization should wait as late as possible. Modern society needs specialists, but for society to keep together despite the disintegrative forces presented by specialization it is essential that all students have some understanding of the subject fields outside their own departments. This understanding is also necessary in view of the increased mobility of the labour market, which requires a general background that makes rapid adjustments to new occupations possible.

The common subjects for all students in the first year of the Gymnasium are: religion, Danish with Swedish and Norwegian, English (or German), French (or Russian), Roman and Greek culture, history, geography, mathematics, physical exercises, music and some arts. The special subjects in the language line will be Latin and German, and in the mathematical line, physics and chemistry.

37. Cf. Betænkning nr. 269: *Det nye Gymnasium* (Copenhagen, 1960).

Most of these subjects are continued in the following two years. But by reducing the number of periods in some subjects, increasing the numbers of periods in others, and adding new subjects to the curriculum, a specialization into branches is introduced in the second year. The modern languages line, for instance, strengthens English and German and reduces Latin, geography and history; and the two social science branches add elements of sociology, economics, law, and political science, and reduce the periods assigned to other subjects.

The content of the Gymnasium today is the product of a thoroughly considered plan to establish a feasible balance between general and specialized education.[38] As can be seen, there is no streaming or specialization in the *Real* department. Only when students transfer to the first grade of the Gymnasium do they decide whether to emphasize mathematical or language subjects in broad outline; and then they still have one year to consider the final choice among the branches. Although the choice of a branch does not restrict the student in his choice of future studies, each branch does have its own particular use. The biological branch is especially helpful as a preparation for medical studies, biology, dentistry, and veterinary surgery; the two social science branches, for studies of economics, sociology, history, and law; and the mathematical-physical branch, for prospective engineering or science students. However, the student is free to follow any of these studies, no matter which branch of the Gymnasium he has previously selected.

Another essential feature stressed in the new curriculum of the Gymnasium is the widening of the previous narrow preoccupation with Western European and North American culture to include cultures of other parts of the world.

38. *Ibid.*, p. 17.

Youngsters are taught to think of themselves not just as Danes, Scandinavians, or Europeans, but as members of a community embracing all the peoples of the earth.[39]

Organization of the Schoolwork

Daily school hours for pupils in the Folkschool and the Gymnasium are ordinarily from 8 a.m. until 2 p.m. The school day is broken up into six periods of fifty minutes each. Often the second period continues right after the first, a lunch break of twenty to twenty-five minutes is provided between the third and fourth period, and a ten-minute recess between the other periods. Saturday is a normal school day. Annual holidays are somewhat shorter than in Canada. Summer vacation is usually seven weeks (June 22 until August 12) and pupils return to school the Wednesday after Easter. The pupils are assigned homework, which in the upper grades of the *Real* department may amount to an average of two hours a day; more homework is demanded in the Gymnasium.

Examinations in Secondary Schools

The *Real-* and *Studentereksamen* are not based on standardized objective tests. Candidates all over Denmark, however, are given the same set of papers to write, the same problems to solve. Each paper is examined by two moderators appointed by the Ministry of Education, and normally drawn from teachers from other schools, the universities, and teacher training colleges. The oral examination is conducted by the candidate's own teacher and includes a translation, a discussion, or exposition over a ten- to twenty-minute period. A moderator appointed by the Ministry of Education also takes part in the evaluation of this performance. This moderator must have approved the questions the teacher intends to ask the candidate. The

39. *Ibid.*, pp. 17–18.

candidate's final mark is made up of an average of marks given for the whole year's performance in class for each subject and the marks obtained at the examination.

The great majority of secondary school students are enrolled in municipal schools. Of the total number of children in Danish schools in 1964–65, which was 674,000, only 45,000, or 6.6 per cent, were enrolled in private schools.[40] Some of the *Real* pupils, however, are enrolled in the *Real* department of one of the state Gymnasiums, and hence can be said to attend a state school. Instruction in state and municipal schools is, of course, free.

Teacher Training for Primary and Lower Secondary Education

Teachers in the Folkschool all have the same fundamental training. They are usually graduates of teacher training colleges which qualify them to teach all grades from primary school through Grade 10 or the third year of the *Real* course.[41] In most schools every teacher teaches in the youngest primary grades as well as in the secondary departments. The teacher training course generally takes three years for graduates of the Gymnasium and from four to five years for other students.[42] The Danish Parliament is at present discussing a bill dealing with a major reform of teacher training.[43] The bill calls for a stiffening of the entry requirements, a deeper penetration into certain subject fields, and a wider study of educational theory and psychology.

In the past few years especially it has become increasingly

40. *Skole-, Klasse- og Elevstatistik 1964/65 for Folke- og Gymnasieskole.*
41. Lov om Folkeskolen, para. 23.
42. Lov nr. 220 af 11 Juni, 1954 om Uddannelse af Lærere til Folkeskolen. (The five-year course includes one year in a preparatory class.)
43. Forslag til Lov om Uddannelse af Lærere til Folkeskolen. Folketingsåret 1965–66.

difficult for teachers to keep up with the rapid development of the subjects in the upper grades of the Folkschool. Time after time they have to return, therefore, to attend courses offered by the College for the Advanced Training of Teachers.[44] This College offers one-year courses on the university level in most of the subjects of the Folkschool and in psychology and instruction of exceptional and handicapped children. Teachers may obtain leave to attend these courses, in which case their substitutes often will be paid by the government. The teachers may also attend most of the same courses, however, at one of the provincial departments of the College. It is impressive that every year no less than about one-quarter of all teachers of the Folkschool are engaged in some sort of course activity under the auspices of the College for the Advanced Training of Teachers. This is especially impressive in view of the fact that there is often no direct advantage to the teachers in the form of remuneration or the like that might invite them to take on themselves this extra load of work.

Graduates of the teacher training colleges are not licensed to teach in the Gymnasium. To become an *adjunkt* and later a *lektor* in the Gymnasium one must have graduated from either the arts or the science faculty of one of the universities;[45] this course ordinarily takes seven to eight years. The university student majors in one of the subjects of the Gymnasium and takes another as an additional subject. He may, for example, study English as his main subject and history as his second subject. The subject of English, however, involves more than just the language. It is philology and English history, literature, and social affairs; in short, English or Anglo-American culture. In addition, the degree prepares the student to carry out independent research in his chosen field. Education, though, is not a subject in the

44. i.e., Danmarks Lærerhøjskole.
45. Lov om Gymnasieskoler, para. 16.

university course. The educational practice and theory required[46] of the young teacher are provided by in-service training in combination with a brief theoretical course leading to the *examen paedagogicum*. This is usually held one year after graduation.

CONCLUDING REMARKS

You have probably found the structure of our education system very different from the fine pattern you have woven yourselves. In concluding this opening lecture, I should therefore like to return to my introductory remarks. You may have found it impressive that an eighteen-year-old candidate for the *Studentereksamen* has behind him seven years' study of English language and culture, six of German, some study of Swedish and Norwegian during at least seven years, four years of Latin, and three of French—this is the case for the student in the modern language branch—and that he has studied his mother tongue, history, mathematics, and the other school subjects as well. You must, however, understand the national conditions that determine this program. We are a very small nation. No more than four and a half to five million people speak our language. Important cultural influences come to us by means of foreign languages. This is also the case with research results and with a wide diversity of material goods. On the other hand, what we want to give to the surrounding world has to be given in the world's languages. To study, to work, to travel, to trade, and to communicate, it is necessary for us to know the language, culture, and thinking of other countries. It is a matter of survival for us not to isolate ourselves.

Not all countries are in the same position. They do not have to pay the same price and can use the time that we

46. *Ibid.*, para. 17.

spend on languages and on study of other cultures on matters that perhaps we deplorably neglect in our schools.

A second national condition that affects our schools is the total lack of raw materials in Denmark. This makes it indispensable for us to rely, perhaps more heavily than other nations, on highly specialized human resources that can compete with the best of our competitors on the world market. We must also rely more on the general education of the common man. I shall devote the next lecture to a more elaborate exposition of this topic.

A third national condition is our lengthy tradition of highly centralized direction of education, which I mentioned earlier. The existence of such an "outside agency" may have made it easier for us to bring about the changes in the school system necessary to adapt it to the changing requirements of society, for the impulse toward most educational change seems to be effected by agencies outside the schools; only to a lesser degree do great educational reforms emerge from within the system itself.

A final feature that has a strong bearing on our schools is the concern of the population for education. The Danish people have a very positive attitude to this part of their communal life. But this, however, is the result of historical development, the slow growth of more than a century. Such an attitude is not acquired by any country overnight.

SECOND LECTURE

Technical Education and Trade Training

Technical Education and Trade Training

AN EDUCATIONAL SYSTEM is a mirror of the society it serves. It reflects the dreams and aspirations of a people. It shows us what people expect of the next generation, and how they expect education to contribute to social change. Even more clearly, perhaps, it reflects the spiritual and material conditions of a nation's life. Normally a community organizes its educational system to accord with its cultural and professional structure. So if we wish to appreciate a nation's education we must at least know something about its people, its natural resources, and its ways of living.

This is particularly true about that part of the Danish educational system with which we are going to deal tonight, technical and trade training. This type of education more obviously inhabits the borderland between school and society than any other part of our system. Before discussing it, we should take a brief look at Denmark and its social and economic background.

DENMARK: THE COUNTRY AND THE PEOPLE

Canada and Denmark are close neighbours. Less than twenty miles separates the tip of Canada's Ellesmere Island from the largest county of the Kingdom of Denmark, Greenland. Perhaps you think that Greenland is a colony, but it is not; since 1953 it has been an integral part of Denmark, with a county's status. Of course Denmark is a great nation, but not in terms of numbers or area, I am afraid. With only 17,000 square miles (Greenland and the Faroe Islands excluded) Denmark is hard to find on the ordinary school globe. And its 4½ million inhabitants do not take up much room in international company. Still, throughout its history Denmark has been remarkably successful in attracting the attention of other nations, for both good and ill.

Southern Denmark, that is, Denmark exclusive of Greenland and the Faroe Islands, consists of the Peninsula of Jutland and 500 islands.[1] From north to south it stretches about 225 miles and from east to west about 250 miles. It is a low-lying country, but not flat. Its highest point is only 568 feet above sea level. There are very long coastlines, so long that no Dane lives more than thirty miles or so from the nearest coast. No wonder, then, that we have become a seafaring nation. Although Denmark is situated at the latitudes that correspond to the southern part of Baffin Bay, the climate is favourable, thanks mainly to the warm western winds that predominate in that part of the world. The average temperature in the coldest month is 12 degrees higher than the average for the 56th latitude, yet we have about 70 annual frost days on the coasts and 120 in the interior. Neither our climate nor our soil is exceptionally favourable for agriculture; centuries of cultivation

---

1. The geographic facts mentioned in this lecture are mainly based on *Denmark*, published by the Royal Danish Ministry of Foreign Affairs, Copenhagen, 1961.

Technical Education and Trade Training 37

have improved the soil radically, but so far we have not been able to do anything about the weather! As a result of the steady improvement of the soil, three-fourths of the total land surface in Denmark is now in productive use for agriculture. The harvest per cultivated acre is one of the biggest in the world. Normally the bulk of the harvest is fed to livestock, and thus converted to highly marketable and highly profitable foods, such as dairy products, meat, bacon, and eggs. There are no great deposits of natural resources in the land. There are no minerals, no useful water power, and no large forests, and with 386 inhabitants to a square mile, you may wonder how we can make a living at all. The soil and the population seem to be the only natural resources we have. The maximum use of these resources is, therefore, a condition for our survival. Let us look, then, at this population.

There are a little over 4½ million inhabitants in the main part of Denmark, about 30,000 in Greenland, and 33,000 in the Faroe Islands. This population is very homogeneous in race, culture, and language. The language is quite distinct from English, German, French, and other European languages, but close enough to Norwegian and Swedish to be understood by most people on the Scandinavian peninsula. (Some Americans who have heard our tongue spoken question whether it is a language at all; they say it sounds more like a throat disease!) Twenty-seven per cent of Denmark's total population lives in the capital, Copenhagen, a city of 1.2 million; 30 per cent lives in provincial towns and suburbs, and 43 per cent in rural districts. The population is growing steadily, not because of a particularly high birth rate—it is only 18 per thousand—but chiefly because of the low death rate. By the turn of the next century, we expect that the population will reach 6 million.

How do we Danes earn our living? To begin with, out of the total population of about 4½ million only 2 million, less than half the total, make up the active labour force. Of the 2½ million who are not active in production, half are children and students, one-third are housewives, and nearly one-fifth are people over the normal productive age.[2] The 2 million active workers, however, accounted for a net national income of 1,240 Canadian dollars per capita in 1961. This is somewhat lower than the 1,564 dollars per capita which made up the national wealth of Canada in the same year.[3] Contrary to what you might expect, only 18 per cent of the 2 million Danes who were active in production in 1960 worked in farming and fishing. More than twice as many, 38 per cent, worked in the manufacturing and building trades, and 44 per cent worked in the service group, including commerce, transport, administration, professional and other services.[4] The active farming population has decreased very rapidly over the past years and this trend is expected to continue.

This predominance of industrial workers is a factor of major importance for education in Denmark. The towns are taking over more and more farming land, and that part of the population engaged in urban occupations continues to increase at the expense of farming. Farming is still an important employer in Denmark, but we are faced with the problem of producing more and more food with fewer and fewer people on less and less acreage.[5] This is only possible by very close coordination of practical farming, agricultural education, and agricultural research, with a view to still more intensive use of the remaining arable land. This coordination has made it possible, in the face of decreasing manpower, to double the productivity per acre since 1915 and to quadruple it since 1875.

2. *Statistisk Årbog 1963–64* (Copenhagen: Det statistiske Departement, 1964), pp. 50–51.
3. *Ibid.*, p. 518.   4. *Ibid.*, pp. 50–51.
5. S. Tovborg Jensen in *Denmark* (Copenhagen: Royal Danish Ministry of Foreign Affairs, 1961), p. 270.

Technical Education and Trade Training

Our manufacturing industry is very young. It was only after World War I that we realized that Denmark, despite its shortage of natural power sources and of raw materials, had to develop a strong and viable manufacturing industry. Since then, however, this industry has developed to the point where it now exceeds agricultural export, and accounts for a bigger contribution to the gross national income than any other part of the economy. The biggest industrial group is iron and metal working, including engineering. In spite of the fact that all the raw materials used, as well as fuel, must be imported, this group accounts for about one-third of the total value of industrial production. Highly developed and specialized machinery, ships, and transport equipment are among the main products of this industry. Another very large industry is that concerned with the production of food, beverages, and tobacco. The products of this industry, especially canned meat and fish, and of course beer, together with our dairy products, are found on the shelves of most Canadian stores. (This fact contributes to the impression of Denmark as a predominantly agricultural country.) Other vital industries are our textile, clothing and footwear, wood and furniture, chemical, pharmaceutical, electronic, and paper and graphic industries. Only by virtue of a highly developed program of trades and technical education is this very diverse industry able to compete with nations which have more convenient access to raw materials and power.

One last point to be made about Denmark is that the distribution of wealth is fairly uniform. There are not many really rich people, as you in America understand it; but neither are there many extremely poor people. Denmark has been well described by one of our great poets as a country where "few have too much and fewer too little."

Such, in brief, is the society that our educational system must serve. It is a society that, as you are well aware, has been subject to immense changes over the past decades. The transition from a predominantly agrarian society to a highly developed industrial society has been painful. And these developments are not by any means at an end. Such changes must necessarily be reflected in a country's educational system. Our junior school, for example, was designed primarily for the purposes and conditions of an agrarian society. It had to be changed to meet the requirements of an industrial and urbanized society. Our secondary school had been designed for a minority, a small elite that would occupy the leading positions of society. It had to be changed to meet industry's need for unlimited numbers of individuals with advanced training. It had to be changed to answer the increasing demands of families who wanted expanded and improved educational facilities for their youngsters, and who now also could afford to allow them an extended period of schooling.

No field of education is so susceptible to social change as is technical education and trade training. The reforms that are now being carried out within this large and varied field are so comprehensive and occur at such a rate that what I say here tonight will be only a snapshot of the present situation. I should like to deal separately with the training of workers for trade and industry, for commerce, and for agriculture. But let me begin with some remarks about the transition from the general school system to vocational training.

THE TRANSITION FROM SCHOOL TO PRODUCTIVE LIFE

As I emphasized in my first lecture, none of the departments of the public school is intended or even allowed to provide any sort of vocational training. This is true also of those departments which are most closely related to occupations, Grades 8 through 10. Instruction given in

Technical Education and Trade Training

these grades is regarded as pre-vocational, that is, providing orientation to life in trade and industry as well as to life in society as a whole. According to the law on Folkschools, vocational orientation and guidance must be given in Grade 7, and continue in Grades 8 and 9 and in the *Real* department.[6] This is to help youngsters prepare for their choice of a profession or continued education by informing them of the various possibilities and the practical problems in making and carrying out a decision about their careers. They are informed about the conditions of the adult working life, the internal workings of industry, the functions of trade unions and employers' organizations, and basic labour law. The educational system and various occupations are examined, and the youngsters are given help and instruction in discovering their aptitudes and interests. This instruction takes place in the classroom; it is supplemented either by class visits to shops and institutions or by what is called vocational practice. The latter is normally organized in Grades 8 and 9, and consists of two or three periods of one or two weeks each, during which the youngsters work as volunteers in a trade which interests them as a future career, before they decide on an occupation or on further vocational training.[7] This innovation in the ordinary school curriculum has been a great success. Its value as an introduction to the world of work far surpasses that of classroom lectures. Although special agencies for vocational guidance exist within each county, the guidance in schools is given by teachers. Last year, approximately five thousand teachers took special courses to enable them to carry out this function.

Once this pre-vocational stage of schooling is over, and the youngster has left school at the age of fourteen, fifteen,

6. Lov nr. 220 af 18 Juni, 1958 om Folkeskolen, para. 17.5 and para. 21.1.
7. Betænkning nr. 253/1962: *Undervisningsvejledning for Folkeskolen.*

or sixteen, he faces a diversity of occupational possibilities. If, however, he heads for a job within trade and industry other than those that require either administrative or academic training, or no education at all, the most usual next step is to apprentice to some trade or to attend one of the many recently introduced technical courses.

APPRENTICESHIP IN TRADE AND INDUSTRY

Apprenticeship is still the main road to skilled labour jobs in Denmark. Many of our trades have their origin in the Middle Ages, and the apprenticeship method of training new recruits is as old as the trades themselves. Apprenticeship can be served in about 150 accepted trades in Denmark. About 45 per cent of school leavers in the fourteen- to eighteen-year age group enter an apprenticeship. A couple of years ago there were 72,500 registered apprentices, almost half of them trained in the metal industries (such as mechanics, machinists), and one-third in various building trades.[8]

Normally the total training takes three-and-a-half to four-and-a-half years, depending on the trade. Under the Apprenticeship Act of 1956, the employer who engages a person under eighteen as an apprentice must ordinarily sign a written contract.[9] Generally the employer must have been trained in the trade himself, or someone in his service who has been must act as the trainee's principal. Within each trade, a trade committee decides which establishments meet the requirements of the Act, and also works out the training program for that trade. The program is organized as a "sandwich" course, that is, with alternating periods in the employer's work shop and in school. In some trades,

8. "Det 9 Nordiske Yrkesskolemøde." In *Undervisningen i Danmark* (Copenhagen: Undervisningsministeriet, 1964).
9. Lov om Lærlinge af 2 Okt., 1956, para. 1.

Technical Education and Trade Training

training begins with a two- or three-month introductory course in a technical school. After this, the trainee assists his master in the work of the establishment; the master is responsible for the trainee learning his trade as fully as possible. Once a year the trainee returns to the technical school for further theoretical instruction in subjects related to the trade. These courses rarely extend to more than one or two months per year. The employer pays the trainee an ordinary wage while he attends the course. At the conclusion of the training period, the apprentice produces a journey-work and passes the journeyman's test.

A subject of much discussion in Denmark is whether we should discard this apprenticeship system and let the technical schools take over the main responsibility for the training of mechanics, bricklayers, tailors, etc. We might then be able to make the training period more efficient, as the trainee would not have to waste time on the many trivial jobs that masters and senior journeymen traditionally assign to apprentices. It would also be possible to add to the training program an extended course in subjects other than those most closely related to the trade training, so that the student's general education would not cease on leaving the Folkschool.

The latter objective can, however, be equally well attained if the student stays in school as long as possible before taking up his apprenticeship—which indeed is what trade and industry keep recommending to the youngsters. On the question of whether the apprentice's time is being exploited, one might mention that employers are liable to pay compensation if insufficient care in the training of an apprentice leads to his inability to pass the journeyman's test. Many believe also that there is far more educative value in working on the job under the personal supervision and guidance of an experienced master than there is in any trade school classroom. We must remember here that most establishments that train apprentices are very small. Sixty per cent of the artisan apprentices are trained in establishments with not more than five fully trained workers, while 13 per cent of them are in shops run by master and apprentice alone.[10] Most people in trades in Denmark deeply appreciate the wide experience, both financial and administrative, that an apprentice can obtain through this sort of program.

Despite the virtues of the apprenticeship system, the question must be asked, "Is it still sufficient to cope with the shifting structures in trade and industry?" Whatever the answer, the system is not likely to be completely discarded for the next decade at least, although minor adjustments will be introduced from time to time.

ADVANCED TRAINING BASED ON COMPLETED APPRENTICESHIP

Part of the reason why apprenticeship is so attractive is undoubtedly that it offers a very good foundation for further technical education. You will not necessarily remain a labourer just because you take an apprenticeship as a bricklayer or a shipbuilder. You may be on your way to becoming an engineer, or an architect, or to entering one of the other high-status professions that have been based on apprenticeship programs. Another avenue for advance is, of course, setting up your own establishment within the trade. But let us for the moment consider the advanced technical courses.

The most popular and demanding of the advanced institutions a trade certificate can lead to are the engineering colleges.

There are three levels of engineers in Denmark: the civil engineers trained at the technical university; the academy

---

10. Dixon, *op. cit.*, p. 175.

Technical Education and Trade Training

engineers trained at the engineering academy; and the *teknikum* engineers trained at the *teknikum* or technical college. The former two levels ordinarily require Gymnasium graduation or a similar background for admission. I shall return to these two levels in the third lecture in this series.

More than two-thirds of all engineers who are now graduated from the engineering institutions, however, are *teknikum* engineers. This is a three-year engineering course for individuals with a practical background in a trade. Its admission requirements are three to four years of apprenticeship and the *Real-* or *Studentereksamen*, or an extended preparatory technical examination certificate, which can be obtained from Grade 10 of the Folkschool. These qualifications may be replaced by a one-year course in a workshop school followed by at least fifteen months of participation in the practical work of a trade. Before being admitted to the engineering course proper, all candidates are required to attend a one-year preparatory course set up by the technical colleges. The objective of the engineering course is to provide students with the theoretical technical training required for management or independent enterprises. Five engineering courses are offered: mechanical, production, electrical, shipbuilding, and construction. Each of these courses is subdivided into lines and branches of specialization. Besides the purely technical subjects, Danish and foreign languages, accounting, law, and principles of management are included in the curriculum.

An apprenticeship may also serve as a foundation for other advanced trade and technical courses. Three years' apprenticeship in one of the building trades may be followed by a theoretical course for building constructors, and from there the successful student may go on to the school of architecture of the Royal Academy of Fine Arts. Our schools for art and handicrafts offer, among other courses, three-year courses in furniture design and design in gold- and silver-work; these courses are available to young people who have served a four-year apprenticeship in the carpenter or gold- and silversmith trades. As another example, an apprenticeship in the metal industry may be followed by an eighteen-month course for marine engineers.

NEW TECHNICAL COURSES

The changes that are still taking place in the structure of industry are reflected most clearly perhaps in the number of new technical courses set up over the last few years. The changes in industry have increased the need for highly trained technical personnel to fill jobs on the middle level of the technical organization. To discover how these manpower demands could be met, an influential government committee was formed in Denmark in the 1950's and instructed to report to the Prime Minister. The lack of engineers and other technicians seemed then to constitute an obstinate barrier to further expansion of our manufacturing industry. It was apparent that unless our educational system was radically adjusted to meet the requirements of industry our economic development would soon lag far behind that of countries with whom we like to compare ourselves. The task of this committee was, therefore, to scrutinize the problems of technical and science education, and of recruitment of scientific and technical personnel. One of its important findings was that the system of technical education was not sufficiently stratified to allow a really economic use of available manpower. It was found, for example, that civil engineers spent much of their time on routine jobs that could easily be performed by properly trained technical assistants. But such assistants simply did

Technical Education and Trade Training 47

not exist. In consequence, educational provisions for the training of what we call "middle technicians" were set up. Some of the courses are based on previous apprenticeship training; others require only one year's practice in a laboratory. Some are organized as "sandwich" courses, some are not. Length of these courses varies from six months to three years. The demand of the Technical Committee for a more differentiated educational system in the technical field seems really to have been answered. Graduates from these courses occupy such positions as technical assistants (for example, calculators and draftsmen), technicians in electronics and in mechanical industry, chemical technicians, laboratory assistants, and laboratory technicians. A few years ago most of these occupations were not even listed in a dictionary of occupational titles. In 1963–64 a total of 1,500 such technicians graduated from various technological institutions.

COMMERCIAL EDUCATION

Because Denmark is surrounded by the sea and dependent on trade with other countries, we have always been like the English, a nation of shopkeepers. Education for commerce is therefore just as important as for trade and industry, and can claim roots just as old. The traditions of our business training were already established in the Middle Ages and that is why apprenticeship is the predominant training pattern within this field also. The basic commercial training still consists of some two-and-a-half to four years of apprenticeship, served under conditions similar to those within trade and industry. Concurrent with the practical training under a master, the trainee is given theoretical instruction in one of the 200 commercial schools scattered throughout Denmark.

This general outline of the basic training has been maintained, although training of commercial and office apprentices has been recently revised in our country.[11] The main changes brought in by these revisions are the introduction of day schools and of special curricula for commercial apprentices and for office and wholesale trade apprentices. The commercial schools, which in 1964 accommodated about 60,000 students, must be attended by apprentices in commerce and in every sort of shop or office, whether they work in bookstores, outfitting firms, perfumeries, or in public offices. Apprenticeship starts with a ten-week introductory course during the first six months and is followed by four courses of twenty weeks each during the rest of the apprenticeship period. When I use the term "week," I do not mean that these courses are full-time. The apprentice usually spends six hours a week in school and the rest of the time in the shop or the office, taking part in the routine activities. After his training period is over, the apprentice writes an examination at the commercial school. If successful, he receives a certificate and becomes a fully trained shop, commercial, or office assistant. An interesting innovation in the new regulations is that commercial schools in their organization of courses assume that students have attended at least Grade 9 of the ordinary Folkschool. This is a highly effective incentive for children to stay in school beyond the minimum leaving age. Another important aspect of the curriculum of commercial schools is that it includes compulsory instruction in two foreign languages. I have heard that Denmark is the only country that requires such instruction in an ordinary commercial school.

The new organization of the theoretical part of commercial training has been most successful. The initial preparatory course especially has been highly praised by

11. *De nye Undervisningsplaner for Lærlinge paa Handelsskoler* (Copenhagen: Undervisningsministeriet, 1964).

Technical Education and Trade Training 49

principals of the new trainees. This course prepares the trainees to be immediately useful for performing simple jobs in the trades. In the school for office workers, for example, the entire typing course is taken during the initial course period; so are general office information, telephone operation, and letter techniques. Students feel much more confident to meet the practical problems of the job with this brief theoretical orientation as a background.

The commercial part of our education system is remarkable in several ways. It is more fine-meshed than most of the other parts. There is a level to suit every sort of talent, and a type of training to answer every possible need of business life. One of its outstanding characteristics is that it allows especially gifted students to leave the non-academic branch of the secondary school, and still obtain a doctor's degree. Students can do so without passing either the *Realeksamen* or the *Studentereksamen*, simply by making use of the special ladder that has been erected for commercial education.

The possibilities for educational advancement, then, are very good for young people who want to continue after passing the commercial school examination. The next step is to attend one of the twenty business colleges for courses leading to a diploma in economics and languages at an advanced level. These courses are generally given in night classes. The young businessman who earns a diploma from one of these business colleges may proceed to a commercial Gymnasium. The courses here require two years' full-time study (or one year for those who have passed the *Studentereksamen*) and are concluded by an examination at a fairly high level. The curriculum includes Danish, advanced arithmetic, bookkeeping, commercial law, general economics, social science and statistics, business economics, history, history of commerce, commercial geography, English, German, and other subjects.

At this point, the enterprising commercial student may have completed his term at the commercial school, have won a diploma from a business college and have completed a course at a commercial Gymnasium. If he wishes to continue, he may now be admitted to one of our two colleges of commercial science (*Handelshøjskoler*). These colleges are institutions of higher education in the Danish sense of this term; that is, institutions that are centres of research and higher education, the latter on a university level. Their courses, however, are more differentiated than those of the university, in that they have what may be compared to a first degree course, whereas universities have only final or second degree courses. The student in a commercial college may, according to his aptitudes and interests, complete his schooling after a three- to four-year course with a diploma or leaving certificate in commercial science. Or he may go further and obtain the candidate degree in commercial science. If after that he wants to undertake research rather than return to practical business life, he may study for the licentiate degree or for the *doctor mercaturae* degree. (The latter is a new degree; so new in fact, that as yet none has been conferred.)

Although the commercial schools come under the authority of the Ministry of Education and the schools and their examinations and curricula must be approved by the Ministry, a close relationship has always existed between practical business life and commercial education. For the most part, the commercial schools are owned and run by the commercial associations, our equivalent to your chambers of commerce. Practical businessmen also participate in the evaluation of examination papers and in oral examinations on an equal footing with educators and theoreticians. Contact between the supply side and the demand side of commercial training could hardly be closer. That perhaps explains why this detail of our educational system seems to have been so widely copied.[12]

AGRICULTURAL TRAINING

A final word should be said about the training for what is historically our most important trade, agriculture. We have never had a formal apprenticeship training in this field, as we have had in commerce and in trade and industry. But the young boy who aspires some day to own and operate his own farm, or hopes to be a tenant or manager on an estate, will want to learn the trade thoroughly. He can start as a trainee on a big farm of good reputation, and after some time there enter one of the agricultural schools for theoretical instruction. Denmark's thirty agricultural schools are characteristically Danish, offshoots as they are of the Danish Folk High School. They resemble the Folk High School in three ways: they have no examinations, they are boarding schools, and they place considerable emphasis on the typical subjects of the Folk High School. However, their main object is to teach young farmers agricultural techniques and the practical applications of the findings of agricultural research. About 3,000 students now attend the five- or six-month courses the agricultural schools offer. Many of these are foreign students, who come especially from countries in early stages of economic development. Some schools offer an advanced course for interested students who wish to return to the school for a second year.

The drift of youth away from agriculture has had its effects on the agricultural schools. Although these are mainly state supported, many have suffered economic difficulties because fewer students seek admission. At the same

---

12. Erik Langsted in *Denmark* (Copenhagen: Royal Danish Ministry of Foreign Affairs, 1961), p. 274.

time, greater demands are placed on agricultural education. Farms must be operated by fewer hands, and still must yield increased crops so that the farmer can maintain a reasonable standard of living. Modern farming consequently has become a job demanding such high qualifications as a wide knowledge of fundamental machinery, chemistry, economics, and bookkeeping. Therefore, it has been suggested that more solid and attractive basic agricultural training be established. Such training, it is hoped, may help prevent a complete depopulation of Danish farms, whose products are known and appreciated the world over. At present a government committee is drafting the outline of a new training program.

Graduates of agricultural schools who wish to proceed to advanced education on the university level may enter the Royal Danish Veterinary and Agricultural College, and there study for the candidate degree in agricultural science. Many graduates of this course return to the rural districts as teachers in agricultural schools or as agricultural advisers. A very strong tie exists between practical farming and the agricultural college; this tie undoubtedly accounts for the rapidity with which scientific knowledge is diffused and transformed into revised methods of cultivation. It also explains the extraordinarily high crop value the Danish farmers have been able to force from each square yard of black soil.

THE PROBLEM OF THE UNSKILLED WORKER

The existence of the rich and diversified training facilities for trade and industry, commerce, and agriculture, must not hide one important fact: out of Denmark's total labour force of 2 million men and women, about 670,000, or one-third, are classified as unskilled workers. Many of these workers may have some sort of trade training and just

Technical Education and Trade Training

prefer a job that is registered as unskilled, but the figure does give some notion of how many decline the educational facilities that are offered them. This group is going to pose a serious problem in the future. These unskilled workers will likely be the first victims of unemployment: they are more susceptible than anyone else to structural changes in trade and industry; they are more difficult to retrain for other jobs because their foundation of general education is too narrow and they lack the skills upon which a specialized retraining program can be based. A serious step toward solving the educational problems of this group was taken in 1960 by an Act on the Occupational Training of Unskilled Workers. Most important, however, is to urge young people to stay in school and learn one of the many interesting trades offered youth today. It is a promising sign that in fact a substantially increasing number of young students seem to follow this advice.

EDUCATIONAL PLANNING AS AN AGENT IN SOCIAL CHANGE

A few years ago trade and technical training programs, as well as those in commerce, were brought together under the authority of the Minister of Education. The various sectors of specialized vocational education had been previously scattered among twelve or thirteen different government departments. To allow for comprehensive planning for the entire educational system, these sectors have now all been moved to the Ministry of Education.

This brings us back to the starting point of this lecture. I said then that to a large extent an educational system reflects the productive and cultural life of a nation, and that this life determines the organization of the educational system. But while it is true that strong impulses flow from production to education, the reverse is equally true. An educational system is a mirror of present conditions, but it is also a generator of innovation in production and culture. When we assembled all parts of the educational system within the Ministry of Education, the reason was not a purely administrative one. It was because we want to do something with the system; we want to direct its development into promising channels. The effort to plan education for future needs implies a realization that what we do in education today will profoundly affect what happens in our productive and cultural life ten and twenty years from now. Thus there is a perpetual circular movement of influences from production to education and back again to production.[13] This process continues to operate whether we are aware of it or not. But clearly, the country that deliberately tries to capitalize on the forces of this dynamic process and make effective use of them in educational planning, will meet the future with greater confidence. That is why in Denmark today so much attention is paid to efforts to reform vocational training.

13. Torgny Segerstedt, *Utbildning och Samhälle* (Uppsala: Lundequistska Bokhandeln, 1957).

THIRD LECTURE

Post-Secondary Education

Post-Secondary Education

THE SUBJECT of this lecture is one of particular interest in terms of transatlantic comparisons in education. Let me make it clear from the beginning, however, that I do not intend to review completely the comprehensive field of education that is suggested by the title of this lecture. I shall restrict myself to that part of post-secondary education which may genuinely be classified as "higher education." To a Dane, this concept is something much narrower than the usual concept of post-secondary education, and it is also, as I conceive it, somewhat more circumscribed than what is understood by higher education on the North American continent. Since this concept itself is the key to understanding our university system, I shall devote some time to an explanation of what we in Denmark regard as higher education.

THE DANISH CONCEPT OF HIGHER EDUCATION

I find higher education a particularly appropriate topic for comparisons between the American and European systems because it is one where clarification is really needed. Misapprehension, misinterpretation, and false appraisal flourish more thickly in this area than perhaps anywhere else in education.

The organization of your courses, your degrees, your credit system, your forms of conducting examinations; the nature of your bachelor's, master's, and doctor's degrees and courses; indeed, the objectives of your university education and their underlying philosophy, are so distinct from our traditions and practices that very few Europeans really understand what is happening on your side of the Atlantic. To the extent that North Americans realize that a university education might differ from their pattern, our European university practices appear just as confusing and incredible to them.

Despairing of communication, we often have recourse to "translating" our respective systems into the other's language; that is, one system is explained in terms of the other. But this is probably the very reason why vagueness and confusion prevail in this area. In fact, the two systems are so widely different that each can be explained and understood properly only in terms of its own language, assumptions, and traditions. I am glad, therefore, to have been given this opportunity to help clear up the confusion in this field by giving an account of a typical European university system seen in context.

You may remember from my first lecture in this series that in 1850 a major reform was effected concerning the Gymnasium in Denmark. In addition to the modernization of the curriculum to include modern languages, mathematics, and science, it was decided that the *examen artium* (now ordinarily called *Studentereksamen*) should no longer be held by the university, but by the Gymnasiums instead. At the same time, the so-called "second examination" of the university was abolished. This examination was a vestige of the old bachelor's degree and had marked the end of the university's general course of liberal arts preparatory to more advanced graduate or professional studies. As a result of this reform, responsibility for providing the liberal education required as a basis for graduate and professional education henceforth belonged to the Gymnasium. The Gymnasium therefore carries much the same responsibility as the American undergraduate liberal arts college assumes here.

The Danish universities thus were left free to concentrate on research and instruction at a level which in Anglo-Saxon countries would be called graduate and professional. This means that at the age of nineteen our students leave the Gymnasium with what is regarded as a liberal arts background sufficient to begin scientific study immediately. You will have noticed that one consequence has been a very heavy load of academic subjects at the Gymnasium level. Accordingly, a Danish student will be admitted directly into the third year of American colleges on the basis of his *Studentereksamen* upon graduation from the Gymnasium. Another consequence is that for more than a century our universities have not given a first degree, but only degrees that mark the conclusion of six to eight years of university study of graduate or professional type.

This organization of studies rests on the philosophy that brought about the great renaissance of the German universities at the beginning of the nineteenth century. The idea behind this reform was that universities should devote themselves to free and unhampered pursuit of truth and knowledge. Universities should be research institutions, where formal education was associated with research only. Although secondary and liberal education were prerequisites for such advanced training, it was not the task of the university to provide them. They must be provided by other institutions so that universities would be free to dedicate themselves completely to high-level research training.

This new evaluation of the purpose of universities was

instrumental in raising the standards of German universities in the last century. Other European countries followed the German pattern, particularly that of the University of Berlin, and the universities again became a vigorous force in the life of these countries.

This view of the role and value of the university remains. As late as 1964, a report on the administrative organization of the universities carefully defined institutions of higher learning as "characterised by the fact that in addition to their educational functions their activities also comprise research work, and that both these activities are closely interrelated."[1]

This view, as well as leading to setting a lower limit to the educational activities of universities, has brought about a corresponding horizontal limitation in the subjects taught. Many courses found in the catalogue of a North American university would not be regarded as higher education in a strict sense, because they are not regarded as associated with research. Any type of education that does not lead the student to penetration into the scientific method of his chosen subject and to independent application of this method in research would not, according to our strict definition of higher education, be offered by a university or other institution of higher learning. Furthermore, since we are rather conservative in our application of the term "research," this leaves to higher education a very small group of studies compared to the rich variety of the American "multiversity." For example, in Denmark the training of nurses, social workers, occupational therapists and physiotherapists, journalists, domestic scientists, and librarians is not the responsibility of the university but is assigned to special institutions. These are defined with a fine distinction as

1. Betænkning nr. 365/1964: *Den Højere Undervisnings og Forskningens Administrative Organisation.* (Copenhagen: Statens Trykningskontor, 1964).

institutions for "advanced" study rather than "higher" education. This is also the case with the training of teachers for the ten grades of the Folkschool. Their course, which lasts three to five years, is given in special teacher training colleges.

This narrow definition of higher education in Denmark, together with the absence of undergraduate instruction at universities, should be borne in mind in comparing the university education of Denmark and North America.

Our universities and other institutions of higher education are fairly pure specimens of the continental European prototype. The American-style university is a sort of hybrid. During the nineteenth century and earlier, American universities adhered to their traditional model of the liberal arts college. However, toward the end of the last century, American universities were confronted by the fact that an increasing number of students preferred to attend European universities because of their vigorous research activities.[2] As a result, American universities developed graduate schools based on the liberal arts college. But because the Americans retained the undergraduate college and designed a graduate course quite distinct from the European pattern, the two systems are entirely different.

THE UNIVERSITIES

Now let us take a closer look at the institutions of higher education in Denmark. We have two universities and eight other institutions which offer higher education. To this list should be added academies for architecture, fine arts, and music; although these do not fulfil the requirements for research, they are usually included in our definition. A

---

2. Campbell Stewart, "Higher Education in a Changing Society." In *The American College*, ed. Nevitt Sanford (New York: Wiley, 1962), p. 929.

third university will open this summer (1966) in Odense, the birthplace of our great story-teller Hans Christian Andersen.

The University of Copenhagen was established in 1479, during the late Middle Ages, and the University of Århus, the capital of Jutland, was only inaugurated in 1928. In the Fall of 1965 a total of 23,000 students were enrolled in the two universities, 17,000 at Copenhagen and 6,000 at Århus. Both universities have five faculties, covering generally the same selection of subjects, offering the same courses, and granting the same degrees. The five faculties are those found in most universities: theology; arts; law; economics and social science; medicine and science.

What is perhaps of greater interest is the list of faculties not included. There is, for example, no faculty for engineering, for agriculture, or for veterinary medicine. Dentistry and pharmacy are also omitted, although some European universities include them. The reason is that when these new subjects emerged in the nineteenth century, the University of Copenhagen was reluctant to admit they were on the same level as the traditional faculties. They were pragmatic in nature, more practical, based more on applied science. Moreover, they aimed at professions which in addition to the use of intellect required also some physical exertion; all in all, they were not considered elevated enough to join the company of the classical faculties. Actually the university felt it had already gone too far in admitting surgeons to the medical faculty.[3]

As it was impossible to wait for the universities to overcome their old prejudices against the practical sciences, special institutions for research and education in these fields were set up during the nineteenth century. Their standard

3. This took place in 1838, when a common degree for physicians and surgeons was established. From 1785 till 1842 surgery was taught in a separate Surgical Academy which accounted for by far the substantial part of doctors trained in that period.

has always been equal to that of the universities, and the attitude to these so-called neo-academic subjects has changed so much that when amalgamation of one or more of the existing institutions of higher education with the universities was discussed recently, the proposal was accepted on principle but for purely practical reasons was never implemented. However, the new universities to be established within the next decade, including that at Odense, have been planned as university centres; they will include such faculties as are not within the scope of present universities.[4]

Entry Requirements

Anyone who has passed the Danish *Studentereksamen* can enrol in any of these faculties. It does not matter which line or branch of the Gymnasium he graduated from nor what marks he obtained in this examination. There is a significant correlation between the *Studentereksamen* marks and the chances for successful completion of the university course, and as far as can be determined from our present university statistics, half of all freshmen never reach the final examination. Nonetheless, the university does not employ any test or other means to measure the scholastic aptitude of new students, nor does it take any responsibility for selection by estimating future achievements. Thus the individual student is left to himself to judge his chances of completing university. But vigorous attempts are now being made to establish guidance programs to assist students in this important decision.

Neither are the universities allowed to restrict the number of new students because of lack of space. This places a heavy demand on universities, especially now when enrolment figures can double and even triple within a decade.

4. Forslag til Lov om Oprettelse af et Universitet i Odense (Folketinget, 1963–64).

The medical and science faculties in particular suffer, for in these faculties a table, a chair, a library, and a teacher are not sufficient instructional tools, as they may be in other faculties. It has been very hard to maintain the principle of free access during the last two or three years, and especially the medical faculties, in desperation, have repeatedly declared that they would have to introduce *numerus clausus* in order to give proper instruction to their students. The government, however, has firmly refused to comply. Instead, these faculties have been asked to plan ahead and to determine what facilities will be needed to accommodate the expected number of new students, one, two, and more years ahead. The government and the parliament have committed themselves so completely to the maintenance of this principle of unrestricted access that they will ensure that buildings, staff, and other requirements are provided, if only the faculties predict what the needs will be. Last year the Minister of Education, struggling with medical professors over the admission of new students, performed what almost amounts to a conjuror's trick: in one afternoon he raised one million Danish kroner (about $155,000) to prevent any restriction of this principle.

Perhaps it would be wise at this point to warn you against jumping to wrong conclusions about academic freedom and the autonomy of the universities. The question of how many students should be provided with educational facilities in a state university is hardly a matter of academic freedom. It does not imply any right of the government or the parliament to interfere with what topics are examined or what ideas are taught in the universities. It is, on the other hand, related to the question of the universities' autonomy, which it admittedly delimits. But in Denmark, where the universities are owned and operated by the state, their autonomy is mainly confined to such fields as are necessary

Post-Secondary Education

for the protection of academic freedom, or where such autonomy is found to be practical from an administrative point of view.[5]

Another thing that ought to be said in connection with entrance requirements is that university education in Denmark is free. No fees are paid by the student; higher education is a service that the state and the universities generously extend to everyone. The financial risk of students who drop out is partly borne by the state, as a sort of premium paid to discover and train all potential contributors to the future benefit of society. And of course, since most of the graduating students enter the highest income categories of the population, a significant part of these costs will be paid back in taxes over the years.

Degrees and Courses

In all five faculties, the usual course is directed toward what we call the candidate degree. The courses vary from six to eight years in length, depending on the choice of study and on personal study habits. The faculties of theology, law, and medicine confer only the candidate degree,[6] whereas the faculties of arts and science also offer the alternative *magister* degree. According to their chosen field of study the graduates of the most common courses are known by the abbreviations: *cand. theol.*, *cand. jur.*, *cand. polit.* (political economy), *cand. mag.* (the main arts degree), *cand. art.*, *cand. psych.*, *cand. scient.*, and *cand. med.* The

---

5. A more thorough account of the relationship between the government and universities in Denmark has been given in Ole B. Thomsen, "Governments and Universities: A Danish View." In *On Higher Education: Five Lectures*, ed. D. F. Dadson (Toronto: University of Toronto Press, 1966), pp. 86–124.

6. The theological faculties retained an additional licentiate degree up to 1917. This degree has been re-established in 1955, but so far no *lic. theol.* has been graduated under these new regulations.

corresponding *magister* designations are *mag. art.* and *mag. scient.*[7]

The candidate degree is unlike anything you have in your universities. It is a curious blend of an honours course, a graduate course, and professional training. The Latin word *candidatus* originally meant "dressed in white"; it refers to the white toga which was worn by applicants for public offices in ancient Rome. When the candidate degrees were introduced in the eighteenth century, our university courses were designed primarily to fill offices in church and government. Therefore the common degrees were called candidate degrees, rather than the old style master's or *magister*'s degree. The latter was reserved for pure research degrees of the old type which did not lead to office within church or government. Let me illustrate the comprehensive nature of the candidate degree by a couple of examples. The *cand. mag.* degree, for instance, is definitely a professional degree in that it satisfies the requirements for obtaining a teaching position in the Gymnasium. It is also a research degree, since it requires the scholarly study of two subjects over a fairly long period of time, and prepares the student for independent research. In the same way, the law course (*cand. jur.*) consists of six to seven years' theoretical study of the law, aiming at a wide diversity of career possibilities. It qualifies one for a civil service post: by law, a secretary in a Ministry must be either a law graduate or an economist. Our magistrates and chiefs of police must also be law graduates from the university. This also, of course, is a condition for becoming a practising lawyer in Denmark. (In this case, however, because of the theoretical nature of the university law course, the graduate must practise three years with a law firm before being licensed to the

---

7. An exhaustive enumeration will include the numerically less important degrees of *cand. act.*, *cand. stat.* (statistics), *cand. oecon.*, *cand. scient. pol.*, and *mag. scient. soc.* (sociology).

Post-Secondary Education

bar.) So the law course is definitely a professional course, but the university base of legal training also ensures the foundation necessary for independent research in the discipline and this is the case for all our candidate courses.

Our courses for the two arts degrees, however, will need additional explanation, so allow me to return to them.

The student for a *cand. mag.* degree chooses two subjects from those taught in the Gymnasium—Danish, English, French, Russian, German, classical philology, Greek, Latin, history, music, religion, mathematics, geography, social science, Spanish, and physical exercise. (The other science subjects are taught for the *cand. scient.* degree within the faculty of science.) The student selects one subject as his major, which he studies in depth, and this concentration teaches him proper application of the tools of his discipline. The other subject, which takes one-third to one-half of his time, provides him with sufficient background to undertake teaching or research in that field when combined with the methodology learned from the study of his major field. It should be noted that although this course is designed primarily for potential teachers, it does not include any educational theory or practice. Those graduates who wish to teach in the Gymnasiums or teacher training colleges are required to take a brief course in pedagogical practice, history and philosophy of education, and school hygiene before being "let loose" on the students.

Although the scope of the arts faculties is not confined to the subjects of the Gymnasium, only in these subjects can a *cand. mag.* degree be obtained. If you wish to study philosophy, history of drama, Assyriology, Chinese, history of arts, archaeology, educational theory, comparative philology, comparative and general history of literature, Nordic philology or any of the other subjects of the faculty of arts which are not taught in the Gymnasium, you must study for a *magister* degree. This also applies if you wish to study thoroughly only one of the Gymnasium subjects and leave out the second subject. In this case, you must take a *magister* degree in the chosen subject. The main difference between the two degrees, then, is that the course for the *magister* degree is confined to one subject and its study is more comprehensive and less tightly organized than the *cand. mag.* course. The *magister* course is independent also of outside institutions' criteria of useful knowledge. It has no other aim than the pursuit of knowledge for its own sake, to satisfy a genuine love of learning, and to produce a learned scholar. It is probably closer than any other course to what the German university reformers of the last century conceived as university education. Because no direct career opportunities are attached to it, it is considerably less common than the corresponding candidate degree.

The *magister* degree in the science faculties follows the same pattern as that in the arts faculty. The candidate degree of the former, however, is different from its counterpart in the arts. Science students may combine a number of course units into various specialized courses of study to suit their own special interests, and may reduce the compulsory parts of the study program which are not relevant. So far, this is the only faculty that has introduced a plan reminiscent of your units idea.

Instruction and Examinations

Two of the fundamental principles on which the German and the Scandinavian universities were remodelled in the last century were the principles of *Lern- und Lehrfreiheit*, i.e., the freedom to learn and the freedom to teach.[8] The former implies that students should be free to decide for

---

8. A brilliant exposition of the implications of this principle is given by Abraham Flexner in his *Universities: American, English, German* (London: Oxford University Press, 1930), pp. 317 ff.

themselves where and what they wish to study, and more important perhaps, how they wish to study. This freedom is still a dominant feature of Danish university education. Professors give lectures; in some faculties seminars are held; instruction is offered in those aspects of learning that require memorization; laboratory exercises are open to students of psychology, medicine, and science; and books are recommended for reading. But apart from a few compulsory courses in some faculties, the student is free to use these opportunities or not. He may, if he wishes, study entirely on his own, get the required books, retreat to his study and emerge from it six to eight years later to sit for the examination. It is more usual, of course, to attend some lectures and seminars in the relevant subjects and combine these with readings, but no one demands that the student do so. How he has collected the fund of knowledge and the skills in methodology that are tested by the final examination is not the concern of those who decide whether he is going to pass or not.

Consequently, examinations become very important. They tend to become the focal point about which the whole course and instruction turn. To a very great degree they determine what is read and what is not read, what skills are developed, and how the instruction is conducted. Apart from the *magister* course, which has only the one final examination at the conclusion of about eight years' study, most courses have examinations which are given in two or three parts. If given in two parts, the first part is normally held after two to three years' study, at which time those students considered unlikely to complete the full course are sifted out. The final part then takes place whenever the student feels ready for it, three to five years later. In order to ease the examination load a little, some minor courses may be "written off" by sitting for special examinations between the regular ones. Most faculties also require a minor thesis to be produced before the students are allowed to sit for the final examination. This thesis usually requires from six months' to a year's work.

The examination is usually both written and oral. Written papers are of the essay type and the candidates have from three to eight hours to write them. The papers are evaluated by a panel of moderators appointed by the Ministry of Education from university teachers and outstanding experts outside the universities. The oral examination consists of from twenty to thirty minutes of questioning in each subject, with as many subjects as possible gathered on one day; the general idea of these mammoth examinations is that the candidate, on at least one day of his academic life, shall know all aspects of his subject and perceive the relations between them. In the oral examination, moderators also attend the questioning and take part in setting the marks. The participation of these distinguished persons, who may be bishops, justices of the supreme court, or professors from other institutions, is considered a major guarantee to the public of the standard of the degree in question. The moderators also function as a protection for the candidates against unfair questioning or marking. The oral examination is open to the public; this is considered further protection for the candidate. Usually this examination is well attended by other students who want to learn what sort of question a particular examiner asks, and generally see how this whole purgatory is arranged.

I ought also to mention that before he may register for an intermediate or final examination, the student must have passed the *examen philosophicum*. This is an oral examination normally held at the end of a one-year course in philosophy taken during the first year along with the major field of study. This philosophy course is required of all students irrespective of faculty. It is actually a remnant of the old bachelor of arts degree which was abolished in 1775.[9]

The Danish Doctorate

The candidate and the *magister* are the common degrees of our universities, but we do have a doctor's degree. Only you don't study for a doctorate in Denmark. There is no course organized for it. The requirement for the doctor's degree is a scholarly thesis which may be submitted only by a university graduate achieving what we call a First Class standing. The thesis must be an independent and original piece of research that fulfils the most severe demands of scholarly work. If it is accepted by the faculty concerned, the candidate must publish it and then defend it publicly against two critics appointed by the faculty. The defence discussions are usually stimulating intellectual performances which attract large audiences to the university. The doctor's degree is a rare degree, and for that reason a highly esteemed accolade of the academic world. The two universities in Denmark confer between forty and fifty doctorates each year compared to nearly five hundred in Canada a few years ago. The majority of these are in medicine. (An ordinary medical doctor in Denmark is called a doctor, even though his academic title is *cand. med.* The academic doctorate in medicine is a higher degree.)

The doctorate degrees are conferred in theology, arts and science, law, political science, economics, and medicine (*dr. theol., dr. phil., dr. jur., dr. polit., dr. oecon.,* and *dr. med.*). At the moment we are considering altering the traditional demands for the doctor's dissertation in Denmark. Under current conditions it usually takes five, ten, or even fifteen years to complete a doctor's thesis, and that after six to eight years' study for the candidate or *magister*

---

[9]. Forordning 11 Maj, 1775, para. 11.

degree. Many able scholars are deterred by the prospect of spending so long on a single project, and prefer instead to engage in what they consider more active research or practical work. This poses a serious problem in recruiting senior staff for the new universities we are planning. We are therefore considering whether it would be more desirable to introduce a doctorate obtainable in, say, three to five years of intensive study. The quantitative requirements for the dissertations might be reduced while the traditional qualitative standard was maintained. An alternative suggestion is that we introduce a degree similar to the North American Ph.D. and keep our present degrees as higher level doctorates. This would correspond to the relationship that—as I understand it—exists between the Ph.D. and other doctor's degrees of the University of Oxford. It is, however, a very difficult field in which to make innovations; so drastic changes must not be expected overnight.

University Teachers and Research Staff

The teachers in the universities are professors, division heads (*afdelingsleder, docent, amanuensis*—ranks just below that of professor), lecturers (*lektor*), and research associates or assistants (*amanuensis, videnskabelig assistent*).

It seems to me that we are more restrictive in our application of the title of professor than your North American universities. Our professorships may perhaps best be compared to your full professorships.

In Denmark, the appointment of a professor is a complicated matter. Usually a vacant chair is advertised publicly, and scholars who think themselves qualified submit applications to the Ministry of Education (but addressed to the King). The applicant also sends along with his application a number of copies of all his scholarly articles, books, and other publications to testify to his research qualification. On the basis of careful study and evaluation of these publications, a committee appointed by the faculty concerned reports to the faculty on the suitability of each applicant. If the faculty cannot agree on any one applicant, the Ministry of Education sets up a new committee consisting of the old one plus an additional number of Danish and foreign experts in the particular field. If the committee decides on one applicant, this individual is appointed by the King. If it is still not possible to make a selection, the committee may decide that a professors' competition be held; such a competition consists sometimes of a written treatise, but more often of one or more public lectures. These competitions do not occur frequently, but when they do, they are regarded as a major attraction in the academic world.

You will have noticed that the evaluation of a would-be professor is made on the basis of his research abilities. His teaching qualifications may be an asset, but his research qualifications are the decisive points. So it is with most of the university staff. Everyone employed in a full-time position at the university is either a researcher or a researcher and instructor, and is expected to divide his time at least evenly between research and teaching. The younger associates and assistants are expected to use their time in teaching, giving assistance to the institute or the professor, and undertaking personal research. Normally they have between one-third and two-thirds of their time free for their own research; this is how they are able to write the dissertations qualifying them for senior posts. Besides these ordinary positions, the state grants a large number of research fellowships (*kandidatstipendiat, universitetsadjunkt, forskerstipendiat*) which allow young scholars to concentrate fully on a personal research project for some years. Such fellows are not supposed to participate in any organized institute work, and the teaching load that can be placed upon them is highly restricted. Since the remuneration corresponds to that received by a research associate, a high school teacher, a governmental secretary, or other government-employed graduate, these fellowships are attractive indeed, and are effective instruments in recruiting young graduates to a research and university career. The fellowships were established only a few years ago, but have already proved a great success—and I know that many European countries envy us this arrangement.

An Attempt at Comparison

Before I leave the subject of universities, I shall try to answer a question I know you have: "Where does your candidate or *magister* degree rank in relation to our degrees?" By now you know me well enough to know that I decline to make such comparisons, and insist on relating a system to its own environment rather than drawing parallels between uniquely functioning systems.

If you press me, however, I shall first reduce the scope to one university in particular, the University of Toronto. On the basis of the limited knowledge I have of this university, my first impression when I try to compare is that our graduates seem to have a more solid foundation of knowledge related to their subject than perhaps even your doctorate students have in their general field of study. I find it reasonable to compare our graduates with your doctors because their courses are of about the same length. The wider knowledge possessed by our graduates is probably a natural consequence of our choosing a main field of study at the age of eighteen or nineteen and sticking to it for six or eight years. But it is also the result of our emphasis on study as being identical with acquiring knowledge, and of the premium our examination system places on factual knowledge. On the other hand, I am impressed by the superior ability shown by your young academic doctors in research techniques and independent application of factual knowledge. And because of your liberal arts tradition they often—though not necessarily—have a broader view of subjects outside their specialty.

The two systems must be regarded as equally successful in so far as they attain the goals they have set for their activities. Personally, however, I should like our universities to learn from your insistence that students work independently with the knowledge presented to them. The idea of university education as apprenticeship participation in worthwhile research was an idea North Americans imported from the Continent a century ago. Now, it seems to me that to revitalize our university education, we need this idea back in a form adjusted to contemporary reality.

On the other hand, there are students over here who deplore that so much time in your courses is devoted to writing papers. What these students would like is to devote a few years to intensive reading uninterrupted by the demands of this requirement. Such reading would be a preparation for the productive life that starts after graduation. Students who feel this need to become absorbed in their subject are envious of our organization of courses, although perhaps they would be deterred by the rigid, medieval examination system associated with it. It seems to me that none of us have so far found the correct formula to determine the balance between acquisition and application of knowledge in our university education.

OTHER INSTITUTIONS OF HIGHER EDUCATION

I have devoted this much time to the universities because I wanted to lead you deeply enough into them to make you feel what it is like to be a student there. Most of what has been said about them applies to the other institutions of higher learning as well, so I need only mention the latter briefly. The oldest of these is the Technical University, which was founded in 1829 by the great physicist Hans Christian Orsted (the discoverer of electromagnetism and of the metal, aluminum). Here, civil engineers are trained in the main branches of chemical, building, mechanical, and electrical engineering. There are about 2,500 students. The College of Pharmacy was established in 1892. It has close to 700 students enrolled in a five-year course for the candidate degree in pharmacy. There are two colleges of dentistry, one in Copenhagen, established in 1889, and a new one in Århus, established in 1958. The colleges have about 1,100 students enrolled in a five-year course for the candidate degree in odontology. Two years of service as an intern after graduation are required for licensing as a dentist. The Royal Veterinary and Agricultural College was inaugurated in 1858, although a veterinary college had already been in existence for about eighty years and agricultural training had been given at the Technical University. The college trains veterinarians, agronomists, foresters, dairy engineers, chartered surveyors, and horticulturists. The courses are from three to five years long and all lead to a candidate degree in the subject concerned. The commercial colleges in Copenhagen and Århus have about 3,300 students. They offer a wide variety of courses, some general, such as business economy and administration, others specialized, such as foreign trade, banking, accountancy, and organization. Some are day courses, others evening courses. There are also three-year general diploma courses which may be followed by the one-and-a-half or two years of advanced specialized study necessary for the candidate degree in commercial science. In many respects the courses in these schools come close to satisfying the requirements of current views on how courses of higher education should be organized and interrelated.

All these colleges are university level institutions in that they combine research and instruction; their courses are only a little shorter and are of almost the same depth as those of the universities, and their appointments follow the same general patterns. All are entitled to confer a doctor's degree within their field of study. These colleges, however, differ from the universities in one important area, that of admissions policy.

The *Studentereksamen* qualifies the student for admission to these institutions also. In addition to graduates from Gymnasiums, graduates from the *Real* department of the lower secondary school are admitted, provided they supplement the *Realeksamen* with an additional year's study of mathematics and science, or of the special subjects required by the commercial colleges. However, admission to these institutions is at present restricted by the limited number of laboratory facilities.

There are three other institutions which come within the scope of higher education, although they are slightly different from those I have just described. These three are: the College for the Advanced Training of Teachers, which I mentioned in my first lecture; the Royal Danish Music Conservatory; and the Royal Academy of Fine Arts. The latter is interesting in terms of international comparison, since this is where our architects are trained. Construction engineers are trained in the Technical University and architects, who are concerned with the aesthetics of buildings, in the Academy of Fine Arts; their approaches to a construction job are entirely different, although equally important.

THE FUTURE: PLANNING FOR CHANGE AND EXPANSION

Let me now give you some idea of the future developments of higher education in Denmark. When I look at our universities in historical perspective I feel strongly that what we experienced at the beginning of the nineteenth century was a renaissance of European universities. Universities flourished as they assumed a completely new role in social life. Times, however, have changed again, and the effect of this revival is fading out. The need for a revaluation of the concepts on which our universities are based is growing daily. With all that is happening to Danish universities right now, I foresee a second renaissance, one which will shape our universities into forms entirely different.

This whole process started with the post-war increase of school-age children, who moved from the elementary to the secondary schools, and finally about 1960, flowed into the universities and other institutions of higher education. It soon became apparent, furthermore, that this expansion was going to continue. Only to a limited degree was it a result of the increased birth rate. More and more youngsters in each age group wanted a higher education, and within five years the total enrolment in the universities increased 100 per cent. To the government, this increased zest for higher education posed both a problem and an opportunity. In order to make best use of this opportunity, it was decided that a vast expansion of the institutions of higher education should take place in keeping with the growing number of students. A new campus for the Technical University was laid out and money was granted for the construction of 120 new engineering buildings—each of them as large as an ordinary high school—in the period 1960–1970. This means that one new building will be completed each month during these ten years. It was decided also to establish a second veterinary and agricultural college at Odense. As I mentioned earlier, a new university has been established at Odense, and its courses will begin this summer in temporary buildings. A new national hospital is under construction, with a view to improving the facilities for medical education. At the same time all the existing institutions continued to build and build to cope with the expansion.

Post-Secondary Education 79

Soon, however, the situation threatened to become chaotic, and the necessity of a coordinated plan for the development of all higher education was realized. In 1964, therefore, in connection with the bill to establish the university at Odense, the parliament decided that a permanent Planning Committee for Higher Education[10] be set up to advise government and parliament. It was also stated that the Committee should direct its planning on the assumption that by 1985 at least six universities would be needed, as compared to the existing two. This assumption was based on an estimate of the number of students expected in 1985, that is, 13,000 to 15,000 at the University of Copenhagen and 5,000 at each of the five provincial universities. At present, however, this estimate has been proved to be far too conservative and further planning will be based on even larger numbers.

On January 1, 1965, the new Planning Committee started its work. It is composed of university presidents, government officials, representatives of students, and of each major subject field. There are about thirty members in all; a former Minister of Education[11] is their dynamic chairman, and a group of carefully selected educational planners is their secretariat.

The Planning Committee will prepare a plan to develop all segments of higher education, taking into consideration the needs of the next ten or twenty years. In co-operation with the Statistical Division of the Department of Education a thorough revision of the statistics concerning higher education has been effected. All students in universities and other institutions of higher learning have been registered on punch cards; this procedure will give us much more reliable information about the student body than was previously available. On the basis of these data, estimates have

---

10. The Danish name is "Planlægningsrådet for de Højere Uddannelser."
11. Hon. Mr. K. Helveg Petersen.

been made of the number of students expected in future at each institution. A preliminary geographical distribution of the projected increase of students has been prepared with a view to their allocation to future university centres. A special sub-group of experts is estimating the labour market's future requirements for academically trained personnel. Another group is working out estimates of how many teachers will be required to staff the universities over the coming years, and determining how to recruit them.

At a very early stage of the Committee's work, it was found that the quantitative problems of higher education are closely related to the qualitative questions of curriculum content and organization, instructional methods, entrance requirements, etc. The number of teachers required, for example, is partly dependent on the instructional methods employed. The number of students is partly a function of the content, duration, and level of difficulty of a given course, especially when viewed in relation to alternative course possibilities.

The Planning Committee has faced the fact that important steps in the planning procedure cannot be taken until questions such as these have been settled. They have therefore set up a subcommittee to look into the question of entrance requirements. A particular effort is being made to set up uniform entrance requirements for all institutions of higher education, which implies abolishing prevailing restrictions on admission, especially to the Technical University. Also in this connection, the subcommittee is examining the possibility of making early forecasts concerning students' chances of success in a chosen course, and possibly the institution of an examination to sift out unsuitable students after one year.

This subcommittee is in very close contact with another, whose work, because of the perspectives it opens up, is much more exciting to me. The other subcommittee is examining

Post-Secondary Education 81

the whole structure and organization of our university courses. In particular, it is testing a suggestion that has been advanced from many sides, by the chairman of the Planning Committee among others: to re-establish a first degree which might be taken after three to four years of university study. Many participants in the current discussion of this question are thinking of a degree comparable to your bachelor's degree in liberal arts. The subcommittee's terms of reference are not restricted to this one question, however. The possibility of interdisciplinary studies is being examined also, as are suggestions to provide for less specialized professional courses, and for common instruction across the traditionally impassable boundaries of faculties which give some identical courses. It is not possible at this moment to say what will be the result of this committee work. Only one thing is certain: that the committee is composed of people who regardless of their backgrounds are amazingly willing to examine these problems from unorthodox viewpoints, so that whatever they recommend will likely revolutionize the universities—*if* their suggestions are adopted.

Concurrent with the Planning Committee, there is another committee which is looking into the question of reorganizing university administration. Part of this committee's recommendations has already been implemented, namely, setting up the Planning Committee mentioned before, and instituting a National Research Council to act as an advisor to the government on questions of research policy. At the moment, the Committee on Administrative Questions should be completing its second report, which deals with a reorganization of the internal administration of the universities. If the discussions which I followed last autumn have continued on the same line, then I believe that we shall have one of the most modern university organizations in Europe.

Yet another committee is at present reviewing our system of student support. The government annually grants about

$18 million for the living expenses of young people who pursue further education. Bursaries make up about half of this amount; interest-free loans make up the rest. These loans are expected to be repaid within ten years of the student's graduation. This committee is also reviewing the principles determining what portion of the annual budget is devoted to such student support and those which determine who receives these bursaries and grants.

So there is hardly any aspect of higher education that is not affected by the flood of questions released by the first innocent question, a few years ago, about the numbers of future students. There is nothing in the organization of the universities, no unit of any course, no principle on which our university thinking rests, that will be taken for granted by this large-scale inquiry concerning the nature and future of higher education. The inquiry will continue, and its effects will be felt in other walks of life as educationists gradually realize that important decisions about university policies will depend on what direction society as a whole wants to take. A comprehensive revaluation of social objectives thus appears to be one implication of university planning. For, as Viscount Haldane, the eminent British statesman, expressed it: "It is in universities that . . . the soul of a people mirrors itself."[12]

12. Viscount Haldane, *Universities and National Life* (London: John Murray, 1911), p. 29.

FOURTH LECTURE

Adult Education

Adult Education

A REVIEW of what has been said in this series about education in Denmark may suggest that Danish education is overly concerned with accumulating factual knowledge for examination purposes and with preparation for vocational life. This narrowness in objectives and content is one of the main criticisms directed against our school system. A description of Danish education would be incomplete, however, if it were not supplemented with an account of our adult education system. Based as it is on the Folk High School movement, the system has been developed in reaction to the lack of consideration for other aspects of human life that has predominated for so long, especially in the upper echelons of our school system.

THE FOLK HIGH SCHOOL

The Danish Folk High School and the movement it gave rise to, in direct translation called the Folk Enlightenment

Movement, is undoubtedly Denmark's most original contribution to international education. Most of what has been discussed in the foregoing lectures tended to be imported from abroad, particularly from Germany. Little of it can be said to be distinctly Danish in character. The Folk High Schools, however, and the system of youth and evening schools that has been developed to supplement them, must be viewed as a particular Danish answer to a universal problem, that of providing advanced general education for the common, non-academic man.

The Origin of the Folk High School Movement

The Folk High Schools are usually associated with the name of N. F. S. Grundtvig, our great poet, theologian, minister, historian, educational thinker, and "Folk-awakener." Grundtvig was born in 1783 and lived to eighty-nine years of age. He lived during a critical time in our history: in 1813 wars and a national bankruptcy left Denmark torn and depressed; in 1814 we lost Norway, and in 1864 a humiliating war with Prussia cost us Southern Jutland. At this time Grundtvig played a decisive role in rousing the nation to new endeavour and national consciousness. His influence on every aspect of Danish life can hardly be overrated; it has been so great that it would not be possible within the limits of this presentation to account satisfactorily for it.

Grundtvig first entered the educational scene in the early 1830's when the enlightened part of the Danish population was beginning to entertain the idea of a democracy supplanting the almost two-hundred-year-old absolute monarchy. In 1834 the farmers and peasants were represented in the Consultative Assembly established by King Frederik VI to quench manifestations in Denmark of the revolutionary movement which had set the European continent on

Adult Education

fire; here for the first time they realized how far they lagged behind the other social classes.

For centuries, peasants had been deliberately repressed by their masters. Beginning with the last decades of the eighteenth century, serious steps had been taken under the influence of Rationalism to liberate them and to improve their conditions. This improvement required new methods of land cultivation, independent action on the part of the peasants, and a more thorough education of peasant youth. But a people that have been repressed for centuries are not easily awakened. They are not changed into men of progress overnight. The peasants were reluctant to accept anything that differed from what their fathers had taught them. They took little notice of the instructive pamphlets on agricultural techniques that were distributed among them by well-meaning people, and the first agricultural school, established in 1799, did not attract sufficient students to warrant operating the school.

A provision made in the 1814 Folkschools law instructing teachers in rural schools to conduct evening classes twice a week for youngsters over the school-leaving age was not effective. The youngsters had neither respect for learning nor a desire to learn, and the teachers were not very eager to set up such classes. By 1848, therefore, only 9 per cent of all rural schools had established evening classes for youth.

You can understand what a gigantic task it was to awaken the dormant intellectual forces in this farming population. To make the task even harder, the first attempts were based on a completely erroneous approach. The whole Enlightenment movement was conceived in a world and by men too far distant from the peasant population. Peasants were supposed to think in theoretical terms, which they neither understood nor believed in. Since the terms meant nothing to them, they chose to stick to the practices and ways of thinking that had been good enough for their fathers and forefathers.

Grundtvig was much concerned about this widespread ignorance among the masses. He anticipated what would happen when the demand for government by the people was finally answered, as it was in 1849 when our free constitution was granted. If democracy were not to end in sheer chaos, the cultural level of the people had to be elevated. The people had to be "enlightened," as his favourite word came to be, and grow to the maturity required for a democracy to function effectively.

The reason why Grundtvig was more successful than others in rousing the peasant population was undoubtedly that, in contrast to those making previous attempts, he accepted the reality of simple peasant life and thinking as the basis for any future progress. As the target for this progress, he did not want to set up for the common man the cultural ideals of a foreign country and a foreign age, like those of Greece and Rome, but insisted instead on teaching him how to live in the distinctive Danish culture of his time. Such an education, aimed at "enlightening" the ordinary man, Grundtvig thought should be based on the national history, the national literature, and the mother tongue. To him, enlightenment did not mean an accumulation of bookish knowledge, as in the Latin School; it meant an understanding of real life, that is, an understanding by the individual of himself and his conditions of life. Grundtvig wanted the ordinary man to be taught to see beneath the surface of his existence and to perceive the inner meanings of his own being. Learning to live from day to day among one's fellow-beings was basic to the art of being a man. It was indeed the most difficult and significant thing in the world, and in this effort to be a man, the academically trained person had no advantage over the peasant.

In this you will see the influence of great educational thinkers like Rousseau, Pestalozzi, and Fichte. It was only after visits to the universities of Britain, however, that Grundtvig envisaged a high school whose aim was not the training of officials for church and state but the development of a certain type of man—a most important implication of the English word "education." The universities of Britain also gave him the idea of a residential college where teachers and students lived together in a stimulating community.

The school that Grundtvig saw as an alternative to the Latin School, which he called the "school of death," would be closely associated, then, with the ordinary life of the nation. Since it was a "school for life," it would not have any fixed syllabi nor any examinations. It would be as free as life itself and the objects of its study would be all current aspects of individual and national life. This meant basing it primarily on "the living word," the spoken language which, as used in discussions and speeches, so marvellously affected and caught hold of the minds of the masses.

"The school for death," Grundtvig wrote in a famous passage, "is known by everyone in this country. Such a school is any school which begins with letters and ends up with bookish knowledge; and consequently all that throughout the centuries was previously called a school and all that is called so today. For dead are all letters, even if written by the fingers of angels, and dead is all knowledge that does not find response in the life of the reader."[1]

It is no wonder such words strongly appealed to persons who at that time were searching for a new way to elevate the educational and cultural level of the rural masses, and who were anxious to find a new identity for the peasant class. The first Folk High School based on Grundtvigian ideas was set up in Southern Jutland (at Rødding) in 1844

1. Quoted from K. Grue-Sørensen, *Opdragelsens Historie* (Copenhagen: Gyldendal, 1959), Vol. III, p. 76.

and several new schools followed. The development of these schools did not follow any uniform pattern in organization or content. They were also quite different from the sort of national academy which Grundtvig had originally conceived; they were exclusively associated with rural life and their students were peasant youth. But basically they remained faithful to his concept of a youth school for the common man, and he supported them throughout his life. In 1856, at the inauguration of a Folk High School bearing his name,[2] he stated that the sole purpose of the Danish Folk High School was "to rouse, to nourish and to enlighten the human life, which one dare and must assume is in Danish youth."[3] By this he did not refer primarily to a Christian revival, for another of his oft-quoted sayings goes: "First a man, next a Christian."[4]

The Contributions of Kristen Kold

Although Grundtvig was the great visionary prophet of the Danish Folk High School, it was a practical schoolmaster, Kristen Kold (1816–70), who transformed Grundtvig's ideas into practice. Kold opened his Folk High School (in Ryslinge on Funen) in 1851. Through his independent and original ideas of enlightenment and through the personality that inspired his practical teaching, he became the strongest influence on the course that the Folk High School took. Kold regarded himself as Grundtvig's pupil. Like his master, he believed the objective of his school was "awakening" rather than imparting knowledge. Some of the early Folk High Schools had a different emphasis, being more concerned about the "power through knowledge" that the farmers could gain through the Folk High School. But

2. At Marielyst, Copenhagen, later moved to Lyngby.
3. Fridlev Skrubbeltrang, *Den danske Folkehøjskole* (Copenhagen: Det Danske Selskab, 1946), p. 48.
4. The initial words of his poem "Menneske først," dated about 1837.

Kold's view was this: "I must enliven my students before I can enlighten them." Knowledge was therefore subordinated to something more important, the awakening of a spiritual life which would last a lifetime. Kold explained this to a young peasant by pulling his watch out of his pocket, winding it, and saying, "This is how I want to wind men spiritually, so that they never come to a standstill again."[5]

Kold himself was not a particularly well-read man and could indeed be a very difficult person to get along with. He had, however, a great respect for all kinds of practical work, a characteristic found later in the Grundtvigian movement as it developed and spread throughout the country. Since his speeches dealt, not with books and theories, but with observations of the details of daily life and with his highly original interpretations of what they meant to the individual or the nation, his speeches adhered closely to real life. This probably accounts for the powerful impact they made on everyone who listened to him. He demonstrated to all later Folk High School people what the living word could accomplish in rousing spiritual life. His influence on the schools went even deeper than this: under his fiery inspiration a whole generation of later Folk High School teachers and principals was initiated into a life dedicated to the enlightenment of the masses.

The organization of his courses and the content of his curriculum became a pattern for typical Folk High Schools of later times. Since his time, the general outline of a Folk High School has been a five-month full-time course in the winter for young men aged eighteen to twenty-four, and a shorter course for young girls in the summer; the curriculum was very flexible but was usually organized around a core of Danish history, literature, and mythology, and often religious knowledge as well.

5. Skrubbeltrang, *op. cit.*, p. 30.

Impact of the Folk High School

The fateful year of 1864, in which a precious part of Denmark was ceded to Germany after an unfortunate war, became a turning-point for the Folk High School too. What had been lost outwardly had to be regained inwardly. All resources must be united in a vigorous endeavour to restore the spiritual, cultural, social, political, and productive life of the nation. In this movement the Folk High School came to play a major part. "We were christened with the baptism of pain in our youth, and then we became Folk High School teachers," said one of the Folk High School leaders of that time.[6] In the six years that followed the military defeat, no less than 50 new schools were set up and the number of students grew from 400 to 2,000.

In the period up to the turn of the century, when the total number of students had grown to 5,600, the Folk High School had an amazing impact on the spiritual life of the peasants, who gradually developed a new culture of their own based on national traditions. In every parish, former Folk High School students gathered in groups. They arranged meetings, and set up meeting-houses to act as centres for cultural activities in the parish. They discussed political, cultural, and religious issues in the spirit of the Folk High School, and became generators of progress in rural districts. Their members also became natural leaders in communal affairs. The tremendous growth of the Liberal Party—the farmers' and peasants' party—in Denmark in the second half of the last century and its final victory over the Conservative Party in 1901 is closely associated with the spread of the Grundtvigian Enlightenment movement in the same period. It is doubtful also whether the introduction of democracy in local government would have been possible if rural districts had not had such "awakened"

6. Jens Lund, Vejstrup, quoted in Skrubbeltrang, *op. cit.*, p. 40.

Adult Education

circles from which representatives to the parish councils could be drawn.

Another development related to the Folk High School is the co-operative movement; this evolved in the 1880's and has remained a characteristic feature of Danish agriculture. The Folk High School peasants were among the most active in organizing this large-scale economic movement.

Organization and Courses

Most Folk High Schools trace their origins to the same spiritual source and all are alike in their formal organization—yet they do not form a particularly uniform segment of the Danish educational world.

Denmark has about 70 Folk High Schools today[7]; the number of students totals 8,600, two-thirds of whom are women. The schools are ordinarily designed for the age group eighteen to twenty-four and most of the students are between twenty and twenty-three. The figure of 8,600 students in 1964–65 corresponds fairly accurately to 10 per cent of the total number of twenty-year-olds in the same year. In the winter term (which may vary from five to ten months) the schools are almost completely booked; in 1964, 94 per cent of the available places were occupied. In addition, most Folk High Schools offer abbreviated courses of from one to four weeks in summer. These are family courses; baby-sitting service frees parents to attend classes in arts, music, civics, literature, international affairs, etc. It has become quite a popular way of spending a holiday. About 3,000 students have attended such courses each summer in recent years. Six of the 50 summer courses offered in 1965 were especially intended for persons on old age pension.

---

7. The information in this section of the lecture is based on material that was kindly made available by the Director of Youth and Adult Education in Denmark.

The Folk High Schools do not lead to any formal examination or specific vocation. They are dedicated primarily to developing the personality of each student, particularly in its social aspect. The subjects of the modern Folk High Schools are Danish language and literature, history, civics, arithmetic and mathematics, science, foreign languages, religious instruction, and current issues in politics, literature, and international affairs.

The schools are either owned by private persons or, as we say, by themselves. They are not operated for profit but are independent institutions governed by a board in charge of finances. The schools have always regarded as a necessary condition their independence of government interference. Still, they are financed mainly by the state and have since their early days been subject to inspection by the Ministry of Education. They receive grants from the state to the amount of 70 per cent of the teachers' salaries, 3.5 per cent of the total value of buildings and equipment, and 50 per cent of the required instructional materials. The remaining sum is paid by private funds or by students' fees. Such fees, which cover instruction, board, and lodging, will ordinarily amount to approximately $60 a month, and the government gives considerable grants to students who cannot afford this. The normal grant covers half of the fee, but if the student is unemployed or has done his military service it may be larger.

Teachers may be employed in the Folk High Schools without any specific training or without having passed any examinations. Any suitable persons may be employed, and they are in fact a highly dedicated body, many of whom are former Folk High School students. About a quarter are university graduates and one-third are teachers' college graduates.

In spite of these general characteristics of the Folk High Schools, each has its distinguishing feature. Their nucleus

Adult Education

is the pure Grundtvigian Folk High School that follows the ideas of Grundtvig and Kold closely and concentrates on the program which they suggested. But the competing religious movement, the pietistic *Indre Mission* (Home Mission), has found the Folk High School idea useful for its purposes too, and consequently has set up no less than eleven schools. So have other Christian sects and societies. The smallholders have set up particular schools for their youth, characterized by a special emphasis on agricultural subjects but still centred around the traditional core subjects of the Grundtvigian movement. Special high schools have been established for commercial youth, for artisan youth, for young fishermen, and for social workers; and no less than seven schools combine traditional Folk School instruction and life with preparation for training in nursing. The International Folk High School at Elsinore, as its name indicates, is internationally oriented; another Folk High School concentrates on Nordic subjects. The labour movement has set up its own Folk High Schools, and five other schools place particular emphasis on gymnastics and athletics.

Grundtvig himself would probably approve of this diversified picture. It is quite in keeping with his fundamental concept of the Folk High School as above all a contributor to human growth; he felt that the individual schools should be left to develop freely in whatever direction they were inclined. That special Folk High Schools have been set up for specific types of background, for instance, for workers and artisans, is in one sense opposed to Grundtvig's notion of the Folk High School as a school for the youth of the nation regardless of their social and occupational background. In another sense, however, this is justified by the basic concept of associating the school as closely as possible with real life; the reality of life is not necessarily the same for the young farmer and the young industrial worker.

The Folk High School in a Changing Society

Over the past years, the migration from rural areas to towns and from farming to urban occupations has gradually placed the Folk High Schools in a totally new position in the educational system and in society. Originally, the Folk High School was designed to meet the needs of the rural population for advanced education. Up to 1870, when the Folk High School had its great period of expansion, about 60 per cent of the population was agricultural and almost all the students of the schools came from rural areas. In the present century, however, the Folk High Schools have been attended increasingly by town youth as well. By 1945 the majority of the students, that is, 61 per cent, still came from farmers' and smallholders' homes; but by 1963 the proportion had dropped to 35 per cent. When this is considered along with the fact that since the early days of the Folk Enlightenment Movement educational provisions in all areas have improved considerably, we can see that a total revaluation of the role of the Folk High School in contemporary society is necessary.

Such a revaluation has been going on for several years. Because of their independence, Folk High Schools have had ample opportunity to experiment with ways of adapting themselves to their new students and to the new society in which their students live. Some changes have already been introduced. The philosophy and ideals which predominated in the curriculum and whole attitude of the first Folk High Schools centred around the study and romantic glorification of the ancient history and mythology of the North. This philosophy, along with the entire historic-poetic character of the Folk High School, is in process of being replaced by a more realistic view of life and the problems it poses. All schools still emphasize that their key purpose is to "awaken" or broaden the minds of youth to life. But the emphasis is being shifted to match the reality of contemporary life and society. The curriculum has been therefore extended to include discussions of current international and social issues, preferably the most controversial sort. The study of Danish literature has been widened to include modern poetry as well as the traditional treasure of romantic poetry. The discussion of fundamental issues in relation to human life has been broadened to encompass the significance of modern science, modern philosophy, and the social reality of our age, in an attempt to help the individual define a personal philosophy. In all this the dedication to the "living word" has been retained, but the lecture has gradually given way to study groups and discussion classes.

Today's Folk High School seems to be in a period of transition. Important decisions on the direction of its future development are about to be made. Some question whether it still has a part to play in our age. For me there is not much doubt that in its original form it has outlived its role in contemporary society. However, its organizational pattern and its fundamental ideas still seem useful for young people today. The fact that close to 100 per cent of the places available in these schools can still be filled is an indication of this. In an educational system that is too concerned with examinations, vocational skills, and accumulation of knowledge; in a world of speed that seldom provides a moment for reflection; and in a physical and social environment that grows increasingly complex and to which it is more and more difficult to orient oneself—in such a context, the Folk High School offers a period of retreat in which to digest the abundance of impressions that life offers, to accumulate new spiritual energy, and to decide which direction to follow next.

It is my firm belief that as the Folk High School increasingly detaches itself from the ready-made Christian-Romantic ideas that were handed out as a universal spiritual cure to young farmers for over a century, and adjusts itself to the real needs and major questions of the life of contemporary youth, it will have a powerful role to play in the coming years, years which many of us anticipate with some anxiety.

The Folk High School in Other Countries

The Folk High Schools have spread all over the world. There are more than 100 in Sweden, about 75 in Norway, and about 85 in Finland. The idea has been exported to other European countries, to Africa, China, and Japan. Danish immigrants to the United States and Canada also took the Folk High School with them, and established schools on the North American continent. The first Folk High School in Canada was set up at Dalum, Alberta as early as 1917; and in Unionville, just north-east of Toronto, a Folk High School for young Canadian farmers was operated by John and Betty Madsen from 1947 to 1958.

THE DANISH EVENING SCHOOL

The Folk High School is a cornerstone of adult education in Denmark but is far from being its only aspect. As I mentioned before, the Folk High School has had to adjust itself gradually to the needs of urban youth. But in the last decades of the nineteenth century it was essentially a school for rural youth. Its conceptual framework and its emphasis on religious and nationalistic aspects of life had little appeal to the young urban industrial workers. At the beginning of this century the first workingmen's Folk High School was set up. Many labour leaders of the past received their schooling there and it has had an important impact on labour youth. The full-time courses of these schools, however, did not fit well into the economy and rhythm of most

Adult Education

town workers; it was necessary therefore to provide supplementary courses to fill their educational needs.

Out of this grew the Danish evening school. Labour leaders had long been aware that the economic and political advancement of the workers had to be accompanied by a spiritual, cultural, and educational betterment as well. In many ways the workers' position was similar to that of the peasants in the middle of the nineteenth century. The workers were growing rapidly in political power; their economic conditions were steadily improving as a result of their trade unions. But these improvements could not continue without a corresponding cultural maturing of the working class. In 1924 the Workers' Educational Association was founded, and it started a comprehensive program of educational and cultural activities designed for the working class. The evening schools set up and operated by this association have taken over most of the general principles on which the Folk High School was founded. Perhaps their most striking characteristic is their lack of examinations. The courses offered in the evening school do not lead to any certificate or particular vocation. They are established to meet the needs and desires of the population for knowledge and personal development, and therefore these demands alone determine what subjects will be included in the program. This basic condition has been adopted by the whole evening school movement as it spread over the country, and soon other associations and municipal authorities began setting up evening schools on the basis of these principles.

Today, evening schools are run by voluntary associations and by municipalities. Groups related to the Conservative Party set up the People's Educational Association in 1947 as a parallel to the Workers' Educational Association, and later on other political and religious groups took similar steps. The purpose of such associations ordinarily is to publish books and pamphlets of general educational value and to set up and operate evening schools and other courses. But normally the municipalities, even within areas in which one or more educational associations are working, will offer evening schools courses as well. As a consequence, competing schools in the same district may offer the same subjects, with the result that the potential number of students is distributed among various schools; none of them, therefore, have the minimum of ten registrations required for state support. To prevent this situation, the various agencies have started now to co-operate more closely in the planning of course programs in separate areas. There still is much discussion, however, about the value of competition in this field of education, especially as all competing parties operate mainly with state grants.

There are about 3,000 evening schools in Denmark. The courses are normally given in municipal school buildings which are not used by the children in the evening. About 350,000 people, or more than 10 per cent of the total adult population, participated in such courses last year. The subjects they took cover a wide variety of human interests. By and large they can be divided into four main groups: (a) cultural and social subjects like literature, history, religion, civics, psychology, philosophy, arts, and contemporary politics; (b) ordinary school subjects like Danish, arithmetic, domestic science, and a wide range of foreign languages arranged for different levels of proficiency; (c) manual subjects, such as woodwork, needlework, etc.; (d) subjects oriented toward occupational life, such as typewriting, stenography, and bookkeeping, and toward vocations that are not taught in technical schools, such as agriculture, gardening, and fishery.

The instruction must not aim at any regular examination and the only fee is an administration fee of about a dollar and a half, paid on registration. The school year ordinarily

Adult Education

runs from September–October through March–April. The teachers are drawn from among all sections of the population.

The municipal evening school has a special branch for youngsters between fourteen and eighteen years of age, and offers a program especially suited to their needs and level of maturity. This department is called the Youth School; every municipality in the country must make these courses available to its youngsters.

The evening schools also have an upper department called the Evening High School, which the Evening School Law describes as a "school which provides advanced education corresponding to that of the Folk High Schools, aiming at providing students with a personal and social cultural foundation, and based therefore on social and cultural topics alone." A minimum age of eighteen is prescribed for admission to this department. It offers a diversity of courses, often organized as study groups, under the direction of highly qualified teachers. The topics touch on every conceivable aspect of contemporary life. The announcement of the season's programs is eagerly awaited in many Danish homes; last year about 30,000 took part in such advanced courses.

The Evening School and the Future

This evening school institution has long been the subject of heated discussion in Danish education circles. One question I know you will ask yourselves is this: What makes people stick to a course a whole season through when registration is voluntary, when no fee is paid, and when they do not receive any credit for completing the course?

It must be admitted that under present conditions there is a considerable drop-out during the term. But this has *not* led the authorities to consider introduction of fees again. A committee set up to examine the problems relating to the future of the evening schools reported to the Minister of

Education last year. It proposed to respond to the demands of modern life and allow the evening schools to include in their programs vocational training and formal studies for diplomas. As you will understand from what I have said about the foundation of the whole Folk Enlightenment Movement, this concession represents a real revolution in Danish adult education. It is hoped that it will provide an additional spur for the evening-school students to complete their courses.

Another matter that has been widely discussed over the past years has been the justification of state and municipal support for the purely recreational or "hobby-type" courses, such as "Know Your Car," "Book Binding," "How To Be A Better Hostess," and the like. The Evening School Committee has made it clear, however, that the time has come to expand our previous narrow concept of what the evening school ought to be doing. On one hand, as just mentioned, it must open itself toward the more pragmatic and vocationally useful sort of training. But it also has important functions to perform in an age where the leisure time of the major part of the population is being gradually increased. There does not seem to be sufficient reason why one should discriminate between reading Stephen Leacock in English, painting in oil, or tinkering with a motor as worthwhile leisure activities for the common man. In accordance with this view, the Committee has recommended that all courses be accepted as equally worthy of public support. It has also recommended substitution of the term "leisure education" for the traditional "evening education." One implication of this change is that courses should be established during the day as well, to meet the needs of housewives, for example.

The People's University and Boarding Schools for Youth

The resources of our system of voluntary leisure education are not exhausted by the Youth School, evening schools,

Adult Education

and Evening High Schools. A still more advanced level is offered by the People's University. The People's University Association was founded in 1897 as a parallel to the British university extension courses, with the objective of disseminating knowledge of research results into wider walks of life. It has branches in the major towns of Denmark. In the university cities of Copenhagen and Århus, the program includes some topics that are covered by a series of lectures during one or two terms, and others that are studied more intensely over two, three, or four years. In keeping with the general principle underlying our organization of adult education, these studies do not give formal credits, although a student may obtain a certificate testifying that he has taken one of the longer courses. Such a certificate may, of course, be useful.

This was shown by the example of a streetcar driver in Copenhagen. Some years ago this man astonished the nation in a double-or-nothing contest on television with his tremendous knowledge of atomic physics. He won the first prize in the contest, and his examiners did not succeed in finding any gaps in his apparently flawless knowledge. This man had never been to university. He had not even been to high school. But he had studied on his own and had supplemented these studies with a long course at the People's University. One morning, soon after the contest, he left his streetcar in its garage and went to work for the Atom Research Station at Risø.

One final element in our system of free adult education includes the Residential Youth School and the Continuation Boarding School, both of them for young people in the age group fourteen to eighteen. The former is a school that may be set up jointly by a number of municipalities or by private initiative. The length of the courses varies from two to five months and the curriculum is that of the municipal Youth Schools I mentioned before. Just as the Residential Youth

School is a child of the evening school of the towns, the Continuation Boarding School is a child of the Folk High School. It is a private institution, originally with five-month winter and three-month summer courses, but increasingly now with eight-, nine-, or ten-month courses. It comprises largely the same subjects as the Folk High School for young adults. Both schools receive the same grants as the Folk High Schools.

CONCLUDING REMARKS

Adult education occupies a central position in the life of the Danes. Close to half a million men and women voluntarily register for a course each year, but a course that leads only to personal growth and never to an examination or to increased career opportunities. Adult education has become so widespread a leisure activity that many families follow some course at least one evening per week during the winter. This interest may be due to the highly specialized courses in our formal education system, which often leaves a "thirst" for wider studies. But certainly this interest also stems from the tradition founded by the Grundtvigian movement and followed later by the Workers' Educational Association. Many Danes still feel seriously committed to the call to "awaken," to "keep spiritually alive." This is the fertile soil on which adult education in Denmark thrives.

An interesting development is the gradual smoothing out of the differences between town education and rural education. While the Folk High School definitely started as a rural school, it has developed into a school where rural and town youth meet on equal footing. The evening schools, on the other hand, were first set up to answer the needs for the town population. They later spread out to cover every part of the country, rural as well as urban. This mixing of the two streams has so increased the diversity of adult education that the individual has a choice of many opportunities.

It is my personal belief that the future will place still more responsibility on adult education institutions. Our body of knowledge is swelling so quickly that most of what we learn in a formal education program becomes obsolete in one decade or less. We need a vast network of re-education courses, a network that undoubtedly will extend far beyond the limits of what we now define as adult education. There is a tendency also, because of the increasing bulk of knowledge, to confine the content of many degree or diploma courses to the foundations of the subject concerned, and leave the rest for the student's independent study later; evening schools and the form of the Folk High Schools may have a new part to play in this situation as well.

Re-education will not be the only new element in the educational pattern of the future. A constantly changing labour market structure will demand frequent occupational shifts; education must make these possible. The introduction of diploma courses in the evening school, as recommended by the Evening School Committee, underlines the new importance of adult education in this area. In an age of growing specialization, Folk High Schools and evening schools have an important function in building bridges between men; and in an age of growing leisure they can help men derive the maximum benefit from their free time.

Adult education is going to be an essential element in everyone's life. Like Kold's watch, it has been "wound up"; and it will probably not come to a standstill in our lifetime.

RECOMMENDED READINGS IN ENGLISH ON DANISH EDUCATION

DENMARK, MINISTRY OF EDUCATION. *Higher Education in Denmark.* Copenhagen: The Ministry, 1954. Is now obsolete in several ways but is the only monographic exposition in English on higher education now available.

DENMARK, MINISTRY OF FOREIGN AFFAIRS. *Denmark: An Official Handbook.* Copenhagen: The Ministry, 1961. Pp. 848. Covers all aspects of Danish history, geography, and productive and cultural life. *Education,* a reprint of the section on education in Denmark, pp. 237–312, is available through the Danish Embassy.

DIXON, WILLIS. *Education in Denmark.* Copenhagen: Centraltrykkeriet, 1958. Pp. 233, VI. A scholarly work on the history of Danish education, particularly primary and secondary education.

NELLERMANN, AKSEL. *Schools and Education in Denmark.* Trans. John B. Powell. Danish Information Handbooks. Copenhagen: Det Danske Selskab, 1964. Pp. 153. An excellent and exhaustive account of contemporary primary and secondary education in Denmark.

RUGE, HERMAN. *Educational Systems in Scandinavia.* Oslo-Bergen: Norwegian Universities Press, 1962. Pp. 86. (Distribution in U.S.A.: Norwegian Universities Press, 355 North Street, Boston 9, Mass.) A comparative work prepared for the Nordic Cultural Commission. Denmark is dealt with on pp. 13–25.

SKRUBBELTRANG, FRIDLEV. *The Danish Folk High Schools.* Copenhagen: Det Danske Selskab, 1952. Pp. 88. A well-written book on the origin and development of the Folk High School in Denmark and its ideological basis.

www.ingramcontent.com/pod-product-compliance
Lightning Source LLC
Chambersburg PA
CBHW060458080526
44584CB00015B/1467